Training the New Teacher of College Composition

Training the New Teacher of College Composition

Edited by

Charles W. Bridges
New Mexico State University

With the assistance of

Toni A. Lopez
Stetson School of Law

Ronald F. Lunsford
Clemson University

National Council of Teachers of English
1111 Kenyon Road, Urbana, Illinois 61801

NCTE Editorial Board: Candy Carter, Julie M. Jensen, Delores Lipscomb, John S. Mayher, Elisabeth McPherson, John C. Maxwell, *ex officio*, Paul O'Dea, *ex officio*

Staff Editor: Lee Erwin

Book Design: Tom Kovacs for TGK Design

NCTE Stock Number 55057

Library of Congress Cataloging in Publication Data
Main entry under title:

Training the new teacher of college composition.

   Bibliography: p.
   1. English language—Rhetoric—Study and teaching—
Addresses, essays, lectures. 2. English language—
Teacher training—Addresses, essays, lectures.
I. Bridges, Charles W. II. Lopez, Toni A.
III. Lunsford, Ronald F.
PE1404.T7 1986   808'.042'0711   85-31973
ISBN 0-8141-5505-7

Contents

Preface   vii

Unifying Diversity in the Training of Writing Teachers   1
    Richard C. Gebhardt

The Basics and the New Teacher in the College
Composition Class   13
    Charles W. Bridges

TA Training: A Period of Discovery   27
    William F. Irmscher

Linking Pedagogy to Purpose for Teaching Assistants in
Basic Writing   37
    Richard P. VanDeWeghe

The Teaching Seminar: Writing Isn't Just Rhetoric   47
    Nancy R. Comley

Fear and Loathing in the Classroom: Teaching Technical
Writing for the First Time   58
    Don R. Cox

The Literature Major as Teacher of Technical Writing:
A Bibliographical Orientation   69
    O. Jane Allen

The Great Commandment   78
    John J. Ruszkiewicz

Writing Right Off: Strategies for Invention   84
    Mary Jane Schenck

Planning for Spontaneity in the Writing Classroom and a
Passel of Other Paradoxes   95
    Ronald F. Lunsford

Making Assignments, Judging Writing, and Annotating
Papers: Some Suggestions   109
    Richard L. Larson

On Not Being a Composition Slave   117
  Maxine Hairston

Portfolio Evaluation: Room to Breathe and Grow   125
  Christopher C. Burnham

How TAs Teach Themselves   139
  Timothy R. Donovan
  Patricia Sprouse
  Patricia Williams

Contributors   148

Preface

In preparing *The Current State of Teaching Apprentice Activities in Language and Literature* for the Modern Language Association, Joseph Gibaldi and James Mirollo surveyed 248 M.A. programs and 467 Ph.D. programs around the country. These averaged 22 graduate teaching assistants (TAs) each, though approximately 100 programs had 50 or more. Of the programs reporting, 75 percent use TAs as teaching apprentices during their first year of graduate study. In these schools, when students enter the graduate programs, they are almost always given assistantships. Gibaldi and Mirollo calculate that at present over 13,000 graduate and undergraduate students nationwide are involved in teaching apprentice programs, with some 10,368 of these in Ph.D. programs.

The actual teaching experience offered by apprentice programs varies—some TAs work in writing and reading labs; some grade papers; some tutor; some intern with experienced instructors; others serve as discussion leaders of small groups from large lecture classes. But the principal responsibility of the majority of TAs is, according to the MLA report, "autonomous classroom teaching." Most frequently, these TAs teach composition.

Few schools now employ the archaic method of putting inexperienced graduate students in front of a class to fend for themselves. At the very least, departments run orientation programs for new teaching assistants before they actually teach. These vary widely. Some run for one day, others for up to six weeks prior to the fall term. Some offer only practical suggestions for implementing a given syllabus; others bring in theory and allow new TAs some flexibility. Some departments require TAs to take a full-semester training course *before* they receive a teaching assignment. Many departments, however, fall somewhere in between, usually requiring inexperienced TAs to take a practicum while they teach. These courses typically involve instruction in class preparation, essay evaluation, and methods for presenting materials.

What is clear from Gibaldi and Mirollo's survey of apprentice activities and our own research in preparing this collection is that the majority of English departments in this country employ teaching apprentices and are concerned with training them, though few of them agree about exactly how this training should be done. Gibaldi and Mirollo report that the preparation of teachers, even with the recent flurry of apprentice activity in the United States, remains an isolated and often thankless task. Few program directors know the methods of other faculty who face similar tasks; most work out their own techniques by trial and error. Few of those in charge of apprentice activities receive departmental rewards or advancement; many retain inferior status. Yet Gibaldi and Mirollo, as a result of their long and thorough research, say that just the opposite must happen if apprentice programs are to serve our undergraduates well, if they are to provide able TAs now and motivated, capable undergraduate instructors for the future. They call for TAs, no matter what their institutions, to be part of well-designed training programs that are an important and rewarded part of a given department's activities.

Our own experience has been that if efforts to help prepare TAs to teach writing are mixed, those designed to help prepare new part-time or adjunct faculty are practically nonexistent. Yet the same principles should apply. New teachers are new teachers; *all* new faculty should receive substantive preparation for and support of their teaching.

While Gibaldi and Mirollo admit that most major departments now do provide some form of training for new teachers, they find that teacher training is still something that departments often undertake grudgingly and only out of necessity. They find that preparation programs vary dramatically because few faculty members involved with training actually have written about their methods, discoveries, or theories. Certainly, the dearth of articles in major composition journals about teacher preparation bears this out. Until teacher trainers begin to communicate with each other, to work out theoretical concepts about what constitutes good teaching, and to share methods for creating effective instructors, teacher training will remain a hit-or-miss process that departments assign to lower-ranking faculty members and then ignore. Teacher preparation will remain an isolated activity.

To begin to address this need, we asked a number of rhetoricians and writing directors to respond to either or both of these questions:

1. How do you prepare new teachers to teach writing?
2. What advice do you offer new teachers about particular aspects of teaching writing?

The essays we received should offer immediate help to the growing number of faculty members involved in training TAs and adjunct faculty to teach, as well as to new teachers themselves, and we hope they will spark continued and much-needed critical discussion about the training of college teachers. We also think this collection will be of value for all faculty engaged in teaching writing—many of the essays here include substantial bibliographies, and all of them outline successful strategies for the writing teacher.

Any publishing project necessarily involves the help of people other than the contributors and editors. We would like to acknowledge the invaluable assistance of Anne Barva (New Mexico State University) for her thoughtful comments on each essay and of Wendy Farrah and Susan Sadowski for their help in preparing the manuscript.

Charles W. Bridges
Toni A. Lopez
Ronald F. Lunsford

Unifying Diversity in the Training of Writing Teachers

Richard C. Gebhardt
Findlay College

Composition is a complex and varied field, the very diversity of which often poses a problem for any English department that wants to develop a training program for writing teachers. In many departments, the main goal of such programs is helping new graduate assistants survive in basic classes and "regular" first-year courses, though they do not exclude those who teach intermediate exposition classes or courses in technical, business, or journalistic writing. Presumably, too, most English departments do not want to forget other clientele of such programs, as Robert Lyons has described them "senior members of the department who have not taught writing for a number of years" but who are now "teaching composition because shrinking budgets and low enrollments have reduced both the staff and the number of electives in the English department."[1] Nor can composition training programs exclude advanced undergraduates who plan to teach high school English, unless an English department *wants* to surrender much of its long-range impact on America's literacy.[2]

More troublesome than the diversity in clientele is the way that varied client attitudes interact with the diverse subject matter of a composition training program. Whether they are new teaching assistants or senior professors or would-be schoolteachers, the clients in any program will bring with them widely different points of view about what will work in a writing class and what will not. Some will be convinced that good ideas lead to good writing, while others will champion free-writing. Some will be as impressed by sentence combining as others will be certain that more traditional grammar study aids writing. Some will put their faith in motivation and classroom climate to bring forth effective writing, and others will advocate structured requirements and class drill. And all of these conflicting attitudes complicate the central diversity any training program must face—the sheer range of its possible subject matter, from

esoteric rhetorical theory and complex research to pragmatic how-to-
teach ideas.

Completely addressing such diversity is probably impossible in any
one course or series of workshops. But it is quite possible, I believe, to
attack that diversity in a training program that emphasizes unifying
concepts, one organized to suggest an integrated view of the processes
and teaching of writing. Such a program would help its clients understand their own writing processes as frames of reference from which to
approach more abstract ideas about composition and its teaching.

A Responsible Training Program in Composition

Each department will need to determine the shape and scope of its own
composition training program. Among other things, it will need to decide whether to invite senior faculty to participate; whether to offer one
course or more, or a series of workshops in place of a formal course;
and whether programs for undergraduate teaching majors, graduate
students, and senior faculty should be separate or combined in some
way. Similarly, the teachers assigned to develop and run the program
will have to decide how best to emphasize the clients' own writing;
whether to slant the program toward theory or practice; whether to organize the curriculum around a text, such as William Irmscher's *Teaching Expository Writing* (New York: Holt, Rinehart & Winston, 1979) or
Erika Lindemann's *A Rhetoric for Writing Teachers* (New York: Oxford
Univ. Press, 1982), or around issues and themes presented in such texts
as Gary Tate and Edward P. J. Corbett's *The Writing Teacher's Sourcebook*
(New York: Oxford Univ. Press, 1981) or in selections from professional
journals.

My answers to some of those questions appeared a few years ago in
"Balancing Theory with Practice in the Training of Writing Teachers."[3]
There, I suggested that a responsible training program should try to
balance theory and practice in a credit-bearing course marked by four
general characteristics:

1. It should be "a writing course in which students continue to develop
   their skills as writers and become more self-consciously familiar
   with the frustrations, dead-ends, and pitfalls that their students
   will encounter."

2. Second, the course "should press home to students the necessity,
   as a natural prerequisite of their chosen profession, of their being
   writers."

3. "The course should provide opportunity for students to serve as critics of other students' papers—and, of course, to have their papers examined by sharp-eyed students as well. It should do this in a friendly, constructive, but serious climate. And students should see that such activity is necessary, again, as a prerequisite of their chosen profession."

4. The course "should ask students to write *about* the teaching of writing.[4] And to provide material about which to write, it should use readings, guest speakers, lectures, and discussions to direct students to a wide range of approaches and materials."

Just what ideas, approaches, and materials a training program in composition should ask students to think and write about will vary with the sort of program a department establishes. For instance, the Process and Teaching of Writing course I offer at an undergraduate liberal arts college looks very different from the graduate courses that Constance J. Gefvert outlines in "Training Teachers of Basic Writing" and that Joseph Comprone describes in "Graduate Programs for Teachers of Basic Writing."[5] In general, though, I would suggest that training programs use a collection, like *The Writing Teacher's Sourcebook*, augmented by journal articles. And I would nominate the following topics for the outline of a very crowded one-semester course:

Writing Processes

Rhetorical Forces of Audience and Purpose

Writing Processes, Rhetoric, and Young Writers

Productive Climates for Writing Instruction

Grammar and the Sentence

The Basic College Writer

Reading and Writing

Making, Responding To, and Grading Assignments[6]

The range of topics in that list illustrates very clearly the diversity we face when we try to organize training programs in composition. Our profession has evolved so many specializations, so many theoretical underpinnings to instruction, and so many pedagogical suggestions that new teachers are likely to get mired down on their first foray into the composition jungle. What these teachers need, it seems to me, is to develop a synthesizing, unifying point of view on composition and its teaching. And so I would like to suggest that training programs in composition be organized to help their clients discover ideas that unify rather than fragment the way they think about the processes and teaching of writing.

Three Unifying Ideas for Training Programs in Composition

1. *A training program in composition teaching should help its clients develop comprehensive, integrating views of writing and the teaching of writing.*

In "Balancing Theory with Practice in the Training of Writing Teachers," I wrote that teachers need to develop "some theoretical framework with which to sort through the ideas, methodologies, and conflicting claims" of textbooks and journal articles, "so that they can more intelligently develop their own teaching styles and select compatible teaching materials." Today, I believe even more strongly that helping its clients develop integrating perspectives on the diverse field of composition teaching is one of the most important things a training program can do. I agree with Ann E. Berthoff that "without the perspective that theory provides, there is no way of maintaining a genuinely critical attitude towards assignments and courses."[7] The ultimate goal of a training program for writing teachers must be to help them begin, as Frank J. D'Angelo said in a different context, "to identify the most significant principles and concepts in the field which will make intelligible everything we do." [8]

D'Angelo's "The Search for Intelligible Structure in the Teaching of Composition" could, for instance, serve as a place for students to begin looking for the threads that hold our field together. By summarizing and posing questions about D'Angelo's "principles of discourse" (mechanical, linguistic, and rhetorical) and "forms of discourse" (traditional and modern), teachers in training can develop a consciously unified overview of many concepts. At the same time, they can begin to realize that it just might be possible for them to weave many theoretical threads into a coherent pattern. To put it another way, D'Angelo's diagram of the structure of composition can serve as a model of the sort of overall coherence the clients in a training program would try to find for themselves, as well as a sort of conceptual hatrack upon which to hang ideas and developing insights throughout the course.

Other models and other hatracks will, doubtless, suggest themselves to you. For instance, I have found it helpful to discuss with students the contrasting views of composition—"expressive," "mimetic," "rhetorical," and "formalist"—that Richard Fulkerson describes in "Four Philosophies of Composition."[9] At other times, I have asked students to consider the overlapping frameworks of attitudes and approaches in composition—"Product/Process," "Thinking/Writing," and "Classical/ Existential"—that I describe in "Balancing Theory with Practice in the Training of Writing Teachers." But, whatever initial organizing perspectives you may choose, the goal in using them is, as Fulkerson puts it, to help "give a coherent view of what goes on in composition classes" and "to clarify, though not to resolve, a number of the major controversies in the field."

At the same time that students are beginning to develop an organizing framework to help make sense of ideas they will confront later in the course, they should begin to clarify the meaning of a term ubiquitous in composition articles. They should come to see that a "theory" is "a set of *interrelated* constructs (concepts), definitions, and propositions that present a systematic view of phenomena by *specifying relations* among variables, with the purpose of explaining and predicting the phenomena."[10]

The key words here are "interrelated" and "relations." Anyone trying to locate central, unifying principles in a field as diverse—and as filled with competing theoretical positions and specialized research hypotheses—as ours should sense very clearly that a theory emphasizes underlying and interconnecting relationships in order to make sense out of diverse facts and phenomena. They should sense, too, that the theories they study are not objective and pure, but bound up with the unquestioned assumptions (if not outright biases) of writers and researchers. The first section of Richard E. Young's "Paradigms and Problems" is very useful here, especially Young's observation that

> during stable periods, theoretical assumptions tend to function as presuppositions rather than as subjects for investigation. When one believes, he (or she) does not question his beliefs; he *uses* them. It is quite possible to teach and even carry out pedagogical research informed by the paradigm with only a general notion of what the basic assumptions of the discipline are.[11]

2. *A training program should help its clients develop a comprehensive, integrating view of "the writing process" as a complex collaboration of physical and mental activities through which a writer discovers as well as communicates ideas.*

If it is important to help composition teachers discover integrating views of writing, it only makes sense to give special attention to a concept used as widely and diversely as is "the writing process." And there is another reason to emphasize writing process as we try to unify the diversity of our field, since our profession may well be moving toward a comprehensive, integrating theory of the writing process itself, one that accommodates both linear and recursive ideas of composing. This theory of the writing process, I believe, recognizes that general ideas, or initial plans . . . can initiate writing and help carry composition forward. It also credits actual writing . . . with the power to initiate ideas and move composition forward.[12]

If I am right about this development, training programs should help their clients understand the unifying threads running through the diverse models and theories of the writing process. If I am wrong and our profession is split into irreconcilable camps—linear vs. nonlinear, behavioral vs. "thought-comes-first"—it still makes sense for writing teachers to understand various approaches, so that they can draw on them to meet the individual needs of their students.

To help students begin to look for underlying ideas in diverse descriptions of the writing process, a training program in composition could ask its clients to read, summarize, and analyze articles as candidly contradictory as Barrett J. Mandel's "Losing One's Mind: Learning to Write and Edit" (*College Composition and Communication* 29, no. 4 [Dec. 1978]: 362–68) and D. Gordon Rohman's "Pre-Writing: The Stage of Discovery in the Writing Process" (*College Composition and Communication* 16, no. 2 [May 1965]: 106–12). Then, the training program could guide its clients to articles that may *appear* to champion a linear or nonlinear approach to writing but really imply broader views. Here, students might study:

Nancy I. Sommers's hypothesis that composing is both linear and recursive, in "The Need for Theory in Composition Research" (*College Composition and Communication* 30, no. 1 [Feb. 1979]: 46–49).

Donald M. Murray's use of the term "prewriting" to mean all activities that take place before the start of what eventually turns out to be a *completed* draft, in "Write before Writing" (*College Composition and Communication* 29, no. 4 [Dec. 1978]: 375–81).

James Britton's complex and behavioral idea of how "writing at the point of utterance" fits into the apparently linear stages of conception, incubation, and production, presented in "Shaping at the Point of Utterance," *Reinventing the Rhetorical Tradition*, ed. Aviva Freedman and Ian Pringle (Conway, Ark.: L & S Books for the Canadian Council of Teachers of English, 1980).

Reading and writing about such sources, I have found, sharpens sensitivity to nuance in theoretical articles, so that teachers in training can move on to build their own integrating theories of the writing process. And to help them take this step, programs should require clients to analyze and compare a wide range of materials, ever trying to weave them into coherent written statements about the nature of the writing process. It is a very valuable learning experience to struggle, through the act of writing, to integrate ideas from an eclectic reading list, such as the one I have been recommending to students lately:

Janet Emig's work on the interconnections of brain, eyes, and hand during writing, in "Writing as a Mode of Learning" (*College Composition and Communication* 28, no. 2 [May 1977]: 122–28), and "Hand, Eye, Brain" in *Research on Composing: Points of Departure* (Urbana, Ill.: National Council of Teachers of English, 1978).

Barrett J. Mandel's suggestions that writing is something other than conscious thought, in "Losing One's Mind: Learning to Write and Edit" and "The Writer Writing Is Not at Home" (*College Composition and Communication* 31, no. 4 [Dec. 1980]: 370–77).

Nancy I. Sommers's research showing that, as they work, writers constantly sense dissonance between their conceptions and the developing written product and adjust ("revise") to reduce the dissonance, in "Revision Strategies of Student Writers and Experienced Writers" (*English Language Arts Bulletin*, Spring 1980) and "Revision Strategies of Student Writers and Experienced Adult Writers" (*College Composition and Communication* 31, no. 4 [Dec. 1980]: 378–88).

Sondra Perl's concept of "projective structuring," by which writers measure their intentions for a piece of writing and the direction the writing is taking against possible reader needs, in "The Process of Creative Discovery," (esp. 123–28) in *Linguistics, Stylistics, and the Teaching of Composition*, ed. Donald McQuade (Conway, Ark.: L & S Books, 1979) and "Understanding Composing" (*College Composition and Communication* 31, no. 4 [Dec. 1980]: 363–69).

Linda Flower and John Hayes's complex, nonlinear "cognitive process theory" of writing, "A Cognitive Process Theory of Writing" (*College Composition and Communication* 32, no. 4 [Dec. 1981]: 365–87).

The work of any number of researchers and practicing authors who have shown that writing is a process that develops as well as communicates ideas, such as Janet Emig's "Writing as a Mode of Learning"; Peter Elbow's *Writing without Teachers*, especially chapters 2 and 3 (New York: Oxford Univ. Press, 1973); William Irmscher's "Writing as a Way of Learning and Developing" (*College Composition and Communication* 30, no. 3 [Oct. 1979]: 240–44);

Donald Murray's *Learning by Teaching* (Upper Montclair, N.J.: Boynton/Cook, 1982); and William Styron's "Creators on Creating: William Styron," an interview with Hilary Mills (*Saturday Review*, Sept. 1980).

3. *A training program should help its clients use a coherent, integrating view of the writing process as the organizing center of composition instruction.*

Once its clients have begun to develop comprehensive, integrating ideas about the writing process, a program should help them organize their teaching approaches so that the writing process becomes the unifying matrix of curriculum and instruction. And a logical first step in this direction is to ask clients to devise responsible classroom models of composing—teaching ideas that will not mislead students into thinking that there is any single, simple, "right" way to write.

Clearly, any comprehensive attempt to pull the dynamic and hard-to-predict phenomena of writing into a conceptual model is going to be a complex thing—fascinating, perhaps, for writing teachers, but befuddling to students in composition courses. Writing teachers who want their classes to reflect the latest research and theories, then, need to be able to "mediate between the dynamic complexity of the writing process and the understanding, prior writing experiences, and motivations of students in introductory writing courses."[13] And so training programs should help their clients discover how, without becoming simplistic, they can simplify the complexity of the writing process into language and directions that students can come to understand and use.

In my Process and Teaching of Writing course, for example, I suggest that future teachers substitute two words—"intentions" and "processes"—for the single term "the writing process." *Processes,* here, are movements of the hand, observations with the eyes, thoughts in the mind; they are, in other words, mental and physical behaviors that take place, often simultaneously and often with little conscious control, whenever a person is working on a writing project. *Intentions,* on the other hand, are motives that guide writers at different points in a writing project: the need to generate and focus material, to draft for a particular purpose and audience, or to revise a completed draft. This approach (which I explain more fully in "Process and Intention: A Bridge from Theory to Classroom") makes a series of stages the basis of directions that inexperienced writers can follow as they work. But the approach makes it clear that the writing process itself is not made up of any one sequence of steps or stages. And that, I believe, is one of the key concepts training programs should help their clients understand—and move to the center of their writing classes.

Another instructional concept that clients need to understand is that broad concerns of the writing process are not just "theoretical" ideas far removed from daily classroom tasks. In fact, many student writing problems stem from inexperience with the writing process. As Mina P. Shaughnessy puts it, "The beginning writer . . . is ignorant of process, with the result that he usually perceives writing as a single act, a gamble with words." And so, Shaughnessy goes on, "beginning writers often blame themselves for having to revise or correct sentences or for taking a long time to get started or even for not being able to get started at all— problems only too familiar to the professional writer as well."[14]

This lack of familiarity with writing leads to many of the problems that occupy composition teachers:

Sentence-level errors—a fact clients can see by reading parts of *Errors and Expectations* or David Bartholomae's "Study of Error" (*College Composition and Communication* 31, no. 3 [Oct. 1980]: 253–69).

Problems sensing and writing for audiences—as discussed by Linda Flower and John Hayes in "The Cognition of Discovery: Defining a Rhetorical Problem" (*College Composition and Communication* 31, no. 1 [Feb. 1980]: 21–32) and Linda Flower in "Writer-Based Prose: A Cognitive Basis for Problems in Writing" (*College English* 41, no. 1 [Sept. 1979]: 19–37).[15]

Limited scope and effectiveness in revision—as clients can see by reading Nancy Sommers's "Revision Strategies of Student Writers and Experienced Adult Writers" (*College Composition and Communication* 31, no. 4 [Dec. 1980]: 378–88), and Lester Faigley and Stephen Witte's "Analyzing Revision" (*College Composition and Communication* 32, no. 4 [Dec. 1981]: 400–14).

Programs that present such writing problems within the organizing framework of the writing process can help new teachers see helpful unity rather than a confusing array of separate, complex problems.

Besides helping clients use the writing process to organize their understanding of student writing problems, training programs should treat pedagogy in such a way that clients see that many daily teaching activities are related to the writing process. For instance, clients should understand that:

In *structuring a course,* teachers must be sensitive to the fact that many students lack writing experience, and so teachers should require some in-class writing and allow enough time between assignment and due date that students have a chance to complete papers successfully.

In *making assignments,* writing teachers should keep in mind the difficulty inexperienced writers have with audience and offer assignments that make clear both aim and audience, an approach, for example, that Eleanor Hoffman and John Schifsky illustrate in "Designing Writing Assignments" (*English Journal* 66, no. 9 [Dec. 1977]: 41–45).

In *responding to student writing*—whether in written comments on drafts, private conferences, or writing lab consultations[16]—teachers should take different approaches, depending on whether a student's intention in a given draft is to generate and focus material, to communicate an idea to an audience, or to modify and refine a draft for greater clarity and effectiveness.[17]

In *suggesting changes in drafts,* whether in conferences or written comments, teachers should be aware of difficulties students may have moving beyond revisions of words, phrases, and sentences. It is important to give models of structural and idea-level revising, as well as adequate time and guided class activities, to help students learn to increase their range of revision.

In *evaluating completed papers,* teachers should emphasize the record of growth represented by successive drafts and the extent to which the student has moved from generating material, to drafting for an audience, to revising the paper for greatest effectiveness.

Since composition teaching is as broad and diverse as it is, all of us who try to capture images of the field in articles and course outlines should be prepared, like a photographer checking prints just back from Kodak, to find that we have cropped interesting and important things out of the picture. Introducing their four-hundred-page *Writing Teacher's Sourcebook,* Gary Tate and Edward P. J. Corbett talk about the difficulty they had "making selections from the plethora of excellent articles available," and lament having had "to leave a number of first-rate articles on the cutting-room floor."[18] Almost certainly, that same feeling will trouble the writing teacher who tries to set up a course or series of workshops for new composition teachers. My suggestion is that we not become discouraged when we cannot be truly comprehensive, but that we organize our programs around integrating concepts so that new teachers may find some unity within the diversity of composition and its teaching.

Notes

1. Robert Lyons, "Faculty Development through Professional Collaboration," *Writing Program Administration* 4 (Winter 1980): 13.

2. As if to illustrate this point, Charles I. Schuster of the University of Wisconsin–Milwaukee writes: "Every English education graduate who finds a position teaching in the public schools will in some way influence approximately 125 young Americans each year. . . . In time, these students will take their places in society. They will go to colleges, become business executives, government officials, elected representatives. As taxpayers and voters, they will help decide expenditures and policies for education, defense, and the humanities, as well as many other local and national priorities. . . . Yet many English faculty assign the preparation of English teachers an unaccountably low priority." "The Plight of English Teacher Education," *ADE Bulletin,* no. 73 (Winter 1982): 16.

3. Richard C. Gebhardt, "Balancing Theory with Practice in the Training of Writing Teachers," *College Composition and Communication* 28 (May 1977): 134–40.

4. In "The Subject I Writing," I expand on this point by suggesting that the advanced composition course should use writing's unique power as a learning strategy so that, while they improve their writing skills, students also learn about a writing-related subject, such as the processes of writing or how to teach writing. *Journal of Advanced Composition* 1 (Spring 1980): 13–17.

5. Constance J. Gefvert, "Training Teachers of Basic Writing," in *Basic Writing: Essays for Teachers, Researchers, and Administrators* (Urbana, Ill.: National Council of Teachers of English, 1980), 119–40; Joseph J. Comprone, "Graduate Programs for Teachers of Basic Writing," *Journal of Basic Writing* 3, no. 2 (Spring/Summer 1981).

6. For a list of readings I have assigned on these topics, as well as a rationale for selecting these topics and other information about Findlay College's course in the Process and Teaching of Writing, see "Training Basic Writing Teachers at a Liberal Arts College," *Journal of Basic Writing* 3, no. 2 (Spring/Summer 1981), especially 49–55.

7. Ann E. Berthoff, *The Making of Meaning: Metaphors, Models, and Maxims for Writing Teachers* (Montclair, N.J.: Boynton/Cook, 1981), 3.

8. Frank J. D'Angelo, "The Search for Intelligible Structure in the Teaching of Composition," *College Composition and Communication* 27, no. 2 (May 1976): 143.

9. Richard Fulkerson, "Four Philosophies of Composition," *College Composition and Communication* 30, no. 4 (Dec. 1979): 343–48.

10. Fred N. Kerlinger, *Foundations of Behavioral Research,* 2d ed. (New York: Holt, Rinehart & Winston, 1978), 9.

11. Richard E. Young, "Paradigms and Problems," in *Research on Composing: Points of Departure,* ed. Charles Cooper and Lee Odell (Urbana, Ill.: National Council of Teachers of English, 1978), 32.

12. Richard C. Gebhardt, "Initial Plans and Spontaneous Composition: Toward a Comprehensive Theory of the Writing Process," *College English* 44, no. 6 (Oct. 1982): 626.

13. Richard Gebhardt, "Process and Intention: A Bridge from Theory to Classroom," *The Writing Instructor* 1 (Summer 1982): 139.

14. Mina P. Shaughnessy, *Errors and Expectations: A Guide for the Teacher of Basic Writing* (New York: Oxford Univ. Press, 1977), 81. Composition teachers, of course, can have as many misconceptions about writing as their students do.

And programs should give their clients opportunities to become aware of their own writing processes since, as Charles Moran notes, the teacher who is out of touch with his or her writing processes is unable "to test a textbook of program-suggested procedure against experience" and so may commit various sorts of instructional "malpractice." "A Model for Teacher Training Programs in the Field of Writing," *Journal of Basic Writing* 3, no. 2 (Spring/Summer 1981): 67.

15. Increasingly, composition research is showing that rhetorical concerns of audience and purpose are integral to the processes of writing. As I note in "Writing Process, Revision, and Rhetorical Problems: A Note on Three Recent Articles," *College Composition and Communication* 34, no. 3 (Oct. 1983): 294–96, this is a development that makes it easier to perceive unity within the diversity of our profession.

16. For a persuasive argument that the writing process should be at the center of writing lab instruction, see Aviva Freedman's "A Theoretic Context for the Writing Lab," in *Tutoring Writing: A Sourcebook for Writing Labs,* ed. Muriel Harris (Glenview, Ill.: Scott, Foresman, 1982), 2–12.

17. Nancy I. Sommers's "Responding to Student Writing," *College Composition and Communication* 33, no. 2 (May 1982): 148–56, speaks perceptively to this point, and to the whole matter of how teachers should respond to their students' writing.

18. Gary Tate and Edward P. J. Corbett, *The Writing Teacher's Sourcebook* (New York: Oxford Univ. Press, 1981), vii and ix.

The Basics and the New Teacher in the College Composition Class

Charles W. Bridges
New Mexico State University

Writing in 1936, I. A. Richards weighed rhetoric and found it sadly wanting:

> Today it is the dreariest and least profitable part of the waste that the unfortunate travel through in Freshman English! So low has Rhetoric sunk that we would do better just to dismiss it to Limbo than to trouble ourselves with it—unless we can find reason for believing that it can become a study that will minister successfully to important needs.[1]

The rhetoric Richards deplored was one that trafficked primarily in grammar and mechanics, with the basics of writing reduced to correctness, what H. L. Mencken labeled "schoolmarm" English, a set of "gratuitous rules and regulations that afflict schoolboys and harass the writers of the country."[2] All the same, Richards saw a role for a revitalized rhetoric, one that would embrace "the study of misunderstanding and its remedies."[3] The revitalization Richards called for began in earnest in the early 1960s, when rhetoric, and, by extension, writing began to enjoy a renascence.

During the early sixties, such scholars as D. Gordon Rohman, Albert O. Wlecke, Francis and Bonniejean Christensen, Kenneth Pike, Richard Young, and Alton Becker began serious inquiry into writing. Rohman and Wlecke's seminal study of invention[4] gave us the term *prewriting*. Even more important, it gave us an early description of what it means to create as a writer, what it means to develop content in a composition, and how these activities may be accomplished. The Christensens were early investigators into and theorists about sentence and paragraph structure.[5] Their work with the cumulative sentence, for example, provided an early look at helping student writers generate more comprehensive, "richer" sentences. And Young, Becker, and Pike brought tagmemic theory to bear on writing, developing an important text—*Rhetoric: Discovery and Change*[6]—that focused on invention as being at

13

work throughout the writing process. These scholars and others like
them helped start the movement that has served to revitalize rhetoric.

From this ferment has come a redefinition of the basics, so that grammatical correctness is no longer seen as the primary characteristic of
good writing.[7] In 1963, Wayne Booth addressed this question: "We can
offer objective descriptions of levels of usage from now until graduation,
but unless the student discovers a desire to say something to somebody
and learns to control his diction for a purpose, we've gained very little."[8]
This "desire to say something" has emerged as the primary concern for
student writing among many composition teachers. With the main emphasis on content—what the writer has to say—the teaching of writing
assumes increased importance for the student writer, because in stressing content, in requiring that the writer say something of importance,
the teacher requires the student to engage in a process of discovery.

In "Writing as a Way of Knowing," James McCrimmon speaks to this
point, voicing his concern "with a different view of the writing process
[than the traditional, grammar-oriented view], with writing as a way of
knowing, not of knowing in order to be able to tell others, but of knowing
for self-understanding. I am concerned with the kind of insights a
writer gets of his subject during the writing process. . . ."[9] Donald Murray echoes this view in "Writing as Process: How Writing Finds Its Own
Meaning":

> The writer is constantly learning from the writing what it intends to
> say. The writer listens for evolving meaning. To learn what to do
> next, the writer doesn't look primarily outside the piece of writing—
> to rule books, rhetorical traditions, models, to previous writing ex-
> periences, to teachers or editors. To learn what to do next, the writer
> looks within the piece of writing. The writing itself helps the writer
> see the subject. Writing can be a lens: if the writer looks through it,
> he or she will see what will make the writing more effective.[10]

That we should help our students come to value writing as more than
mechanical skill seems indisputable to me, because writing is one of the
most powerful means of learning we can help our students master. It is
true, as both McCrimmon and Murray point out, that the writer learns
about a particular subject while writing. But writing to discover involves
more than this; it goes beyond a particular topic in a specific writing
situation to the writer's discovering his or her place in the world. James
Britton says, "The world we respond to, in fact, the world towards which
our behaviour is directed, is the world as we symbolize it, or represent it
to ourselves."[11] Because it affords both time and opportunity to revise,
writing can help the writer symbolize and respond to his or her world
in a significant way, to order the chaos of that world. Perhaps James

Berlin puts it best: "In teaching writing, we are not simply offering training in a useful technical skill that is meant as a simple complement to the more important studies of other areas. We are teaching a way of experiencing the world, a way of ordering and making sense of it."[12] Helping prospective teachers redefine the basics so that they come to value writing as a way of knowing, of discovering, and of experiencing the world, and allow this view to inform their teaching, should be the focal point of any comprehensive training program. To achieve this goal, a training program should evolve from two coordinates: (1) theory and research into practice and (2) a student-centered writing curriculum.

Theory and Research into Practice

Bringing theory and research into practice in the composition class can enhance the revaluation of writing, not simply because rhetorical theory and research are interesting in their own right but because they provide the theoretical foundation for teaching writing well. All too often, teachers, whether new or seasoned professionals, ask for gimmicks that work—surefire writing assignments, fail-safe ways to ensure their success in the writing class from one day to the next. They ask for a bag of tricks. But when a trick fails, or when a particular situation calls for a trick the bag does not hold, those teachers may be at a loss because they are unable to analyze and remedy the problem. With grounding in writing theory and research, instructors would be better prepared to solve the problems they are likely to confront in their classes.

It is difficult to see how a teacher of literature (or history or archeology or engineering or business or agriculture) could proceed in the classroom without a thorough grounding in the theory and research and in the major texts of the subject at hand. It is just as difficult to see how a teacher of writing can proceed without the same kind of grounding in rhetorical theory and in the major works applying that theory. This is not to say that every writing teacher should study all the works of such rhetoricians as Kenneth Burke, I. A. Richards, James Moffett, James Britton, and James Kinneavy to the exclusion of all else. Such study is best undertaken in modern rhetorical theory classes, not in classes or programs designed to help new teachers immediately with their work in the classroom. Instead, new teachers should be exposed to selected readings that work to translate theory and research into practice.

Most new teachers are simply unaware of the welter of essays and books available on teaching composition. Exposure to such writings can increase or renew these teachers' respect for composing by helping them see that they do have a substantial body of knowledge to draw on. A training course grounded in theory and research, then, can help new teachers come to value writing as a subject worthy of study in its own right and, by extension, as a subject worthy of a serious teaching effort.[13]

A Student-Centered Writing Curriculum

If we translate much of current theory and research into practice, then we begin to develop a student-centered writing curriculum. Developing such a curriculum involves seeing student writers primarily as writers and their writing primarily as the composition course's content or text. Lectures become less frequent; a workshop atmosphere prevails. The amount of writing increases, with students assuming greater responsiblity for their growth as writers. Ideally, the student-centered writing class sends this message: Writing is valued in this class because it is vital. When that message is clearly conveyed, the student writer will be motivated to write. In order to develop this kind of composition class, the instructor needs to consider five aspects of the teaching of writing: (1) process versus product, (2) peer collaboration, (3) assignment making, (4) response versus evaluation, and (5) error.

In the following discussion of these five aspects, I have included a list of appropriate readings and topics for writing and class assignments that I have used in my own training course to illustrate how certain theoretical concepts from research may be approached in a semester-long training course. The assignments are divided into journal assignments, in-class activities, and formal writing assignments.

Process versus Product

One of the most positive recent shifts in thinking about writing is that from product to process, from focusing primarily on the essay to be submitted for a grade to the process during which that essay evolves. Viewing writing as a process is essential to viewing writing as a way of knowing, because it is through writing that students can try out ideas until they find the right "fit" for them, until they find what their writing and their subjects mean for them.

In working toward an orientation to the process of writing, teachers should address such questions as "What is good writing?" and "Why write?" New teachers (and students in composition classes at whatever level, as well) respond to the former question most often by identifying content as the most important aspect of good writing, with concern for audience, structure, style, and grammar and mechanics following, in that order. Discussion of this question actually becomes discussion of the basics; in fact, such discussion actually works to redefine the basics.[14] In responding to the latter question, new instructors touch on the value of writing beyond utilitarian skill, talking about writing as a way of learning, of refining thought, and of strengthening critical thinking skills.

New teachers need to see that there are as many writing processes as there are writers. For many years, texts and teachers prescribed the traditional think-outline-write model as *the* writing process. Such a linear model is representative of the way some people write. But not all. Writing is, more often than not, a chaotic swirl, a dynamic, recursive process in which each writer does things differently than other writers. Here the lesson is that no one process will serve for all writers, a fact to be celebrated rather than deplored. What new faculty need to realize from this is that one of the best things they can do is take a testimonial approach to writing, talking about their own experiences with writing, what they do to write, to get over stumbling blocks, to generate ideas, to revise, to edit. With instructors as model writers and writing models, sharing successes and failures with their students, the writing class becomes less structured, less product-oriented, so that each teacher becomes more a participant in the class than lecturer to it. Such engagement on the part of teachers can serve not only to show clearly that they value writing enough to write actively themselves but also to break down the "them and us" distinction so often signaled by the desk at the front of the classroom.

Readings

Wayne C. Booth. "The Rhetorical Stance." *College Composition and Communication* 14, no. 3 (Oct. 1963): 139–45. Rpt. in *Contemporary Rhetoric: A Conceptual Background with Readings*, ed. W. Ross Winterowd. New York: Harcourt Brace Jovanovich, 1975.

James Britton. *Language and Learning.* New York: Penguin Books, 1970.

———. "The Student's Writing." In *Explorations in Children's Writing*, ed. Eldonna L. Evertts. Champaign, Ill.: National Council of Teachers of English, 1970.

James Britton, Tony Burgess, Nancy Martin, Alex McLeod, and Harold Rosen. *The Development of Writing Abilities (11–18).* Schools Council Research Studies. London: Macmillan Education Ltd., 1975.

Janet Emig. "Writing as a Mode of Learning." *College Composition and Communication* 28, no. 2 (May 1977): 122–28.

Donald H. Graves. *Balance the Basics: Let Them Write.* New York: Ford Foundation, 1978.

Richard Gebhardt. "Imagination and Discipline in the Writing Class." *English Journal* 66, no. 9 (Dec. 1977): 26–32.

James M. McCrimmon. "Writing as a Way of Knowing." In *Rhetoric and Composition: A Sourcebook for Teachers,* ed. Richard L. Graves. Rochelle Park, N.J.: Hayden, 1976.

Donald M. Murray. "Internal Revision: A Process of Discovery." In *Research on Composing: Points of Departure,* ed. Charles R. Cooper and Lee Odell. Urbana, Ill.: National Council of Teachers of English, 1978.

———. "Writing as Process: How Writing Finds Its Own Meaning." In *Eight Approaches to Teaching Composition,* ed. Timothy R. Donovan and Ben W. McClelland. Urbana, Ill.: National Council of Teachers of English, 1980.

Journal Assignments

1. What is good writing? In a paragraph, define good writing. If you have trouble getting started, think about things you've read that you considered good. What made them good? (Another way of phrasing these questions is "What is good writing? What is basic to good writing and to writing well?")

2. Given the proliferation of telecommunications, why should we or our students write? (Or the converse, why should we or our students *not* write?)

3. Respond to assigned readings. (Here the training-course instructor should devise questions to focus the students on the important aspects of assigned readings.)

In-Class Activities

1. Discuss journal entries, developing a consensus definition of good writing and of why we and our students should write, and emphasizing important parts of assigned readings.

2. Assign peer groups the task of structuring ways of teaching writing as a process.

Formal Writing Assignments

1. Describe your writing process. What do you typically do as you prepare to write, as you write, and then after you have written? What do you do to generate ideas and/or information for your writing? What do you do to revise? What do you do when you encounter writing blocks? Compare and/or contrast the way you write with how you were taught to write. How do you account for any differences you find?

2. Outline your rationale for teaching writing as a process, and present representative activities you would use in your classroom for this teaching. What strengths and/or weaknesses do you see in the rationale and activities?

Peer Collaboration

Peer collaboration makes students assume responsibility for their own work in the class and requires them to enter actively into the work of the class. As students work with each other—talking out ideas before and while they write and then after they have written, criticizing and editing each other's papers—the content and mechanics of their writing improve. Weaker students receive help with their writing, and stronger students receive reinforcement concerning the quality of their work in the class. Perhaps most important, they begin to gain insight into the writing process. They begin to see that this process is dynamic rather than static, and they begin to understand the necessity of revision in a substantive sense, as something more than editing for spelling and punctuation. Peer groups also provide a real and immediate audience for the writing, so that writers have a sense of writing for someone they can identify rather than a vast, vague group of "somebodies out there somewhere."

Teachers also benefit from peer collaboration. Because the burden of editing is placed on the students themselves, teachers receive papers that have already been edited, and while these essays may not be perfect, there will be fewer problems with content, audience, structure, style, grammar, and mechanics. In addition, because peer groups are founded on the necessity of revision, students will write more than they might otherwise, so that while teachers are actually grading fewer papers, students are writing more, completing two and three drafts for each assignment.

Readings

> Kenneth Bruffee. *A Short Course in Writing*, 2d ed. Boston: Little, Brown, 1980. See especially part 5, "Collaborative Learning," 103–34.
>
> Thom Hawkins. *Group Inquiry Techniques for Teaching Writing*. Urbana, Ill.: National Council of Teachers of English, 1976.

Journal Assignments

> 1. Describe any peer collaboration you have been involved with in the past. How successful was it? Identify the strengths and weaknesses you associate with collaborative work.
> 2. Respond to assigned readings.

In-Class Activities

> Use peer groups to develop ways to use groups in the composition class: Experiment with groups of various sizes (from two to five); develop sample critique sheets for responding to writing; develop ground rules for using groups; develop ways of using groups in prewriting, writing, and rewriting activities.

Formal Writing Assignment

> Structure and use a peer group activity in your composition class. How well did it work? Not work? What is your assessment of the activity's success or failure? How would you restructure the activity to improve it?

Assignment Making

If our student writers are to learn the value of writing, the assignments they respond to need to be made thoughtfully and carefully, so that each assignment is not seen simply as busywork or as only one more assignment toward completing some arbitrary number. Assignments should be clear and purposeful, and they should derive from the stated goals of the instructor or of the overall composition program. (These goals may emerge from the discussion and writing about process versus product.) Further, assignments should be manageable; students should be able to complete them in the time allotted to them. To ensure that assignments are manageable, instructors should respond to at least one of their own assignments before having their students write, which allows instructors a chance to gain an idea of what is and is not manageable in the context of the writing class and to write papers they may use as models in their classes.

Student writers benefit from well-made assignments by having a clear sense of direction; an assignment should stake out the territory for the student to explore without restricting that exploration. Further, there can be little doubt about teacher expectations in a well-made assignment. Students should gain a clear sense of evaluation criteria from the assignment, which should lay out or point toward acceptable routes writers may take through it.

As they work to develop a rationale for their own assignments and then to write assignments informed by it, teachers need to learn to evaluate their assignments so that they can make adjustments as necessary. New teachers should also come to see the importance of a definite sequence of assignments. Assignments must not exist in a vacuum; instead, each must lead to the next, so that a writing course becomes a cumulative experience rather than remaining a series of discrete essays that have little, if any, connection.[15]

Readings

Eleanor M. Hoffman and John P. Schifsky. "Designing Writing Assignments." *English Journal* 66, no. 9 (Dec. 1977): 41–45.

Cheryl Sandford Jenkins. "The Writing Assignment: An Obstacle or a Vehicle?" *English Journal* 69, no. 9 (Dec. 1980): 66–69.

Journal Assignments

1. Describe the best writing assignment you received as a student. What made it good? Describe the worst writing assignment you received. What made it bad? In each instance, how did you feel before you began writing?

While you were writing? After you handed the writing in? From this response, outline a brief rationale for a well-made writing assignment.

2. Respond to assigned readings.

In-Class Activities

From journal entries, develop a consensus set of criteria for good writing assignments. With this set as a guide, evaluate several sample assignments, revising weaker assignments to strengthen them, analyzing stronger assignments.

Formal Writing Assignments

1. Outline your rationale for a good writing assignment. Then present a well-made assignment; place it in your writing course (e.g., time of semester, sequence in which it occurs, course objectives it embodies); and evaluate it, using your rationale as a guide. What strengths and/or weaknesses do you see in the assignment? In your rationale?

2. Develop a writing assignment. Fulfill the assignment yourself; then assess its strengths and weaknesses. On what do you base this assessment? Did the assignment elicit the writing you thought it would? Why or why not? Revise the assignment accordingly.

Response versus Evaluation

Many of the students who enter our composition classes are apprehensive about their writing. They believe they cannot write and so do not or will not write. In all probability, this apprehension stems from the evaluation of their writing in other English courses. The grammar-mechanics view of the basics produces too much concern with grammatical and mechanical correctness, and some teachers dutifully mark every error on every paper, scrutinizing each word to be sure of spelling, punctuation, and penmanship, mercilessly marking each problem in red. We see far too many students in our freshman writing courses who are writing-apprehensive. Donald Graves expresses well the problem with such evaluation:

> Writers leave the shelter of anonymity and offer to public scrutiny their interior language, feelings, and thoughts. As one writer phrased it, "A writer is a person with his skin off."
>
> There lie both the appeal and the threat of writing. Any writer can be deeply hurt. At no point is the learner more vulnerable than in writing. When a child writes, "My sister was hit by a terck yesterday" and the teacher's response is a red-circled "terck" with no further comment, educational standards may have been upheld, but the child will think twice before entering the writing process again. Inane and apathetic writing is often the writer's only means of self-protection.[16]

Even though Graves is speaking of younger student writers, the principle he advances is nonetheless valid for college writers: as an act of human communication, writing deserves a human response. Teachers must learn ways of responding to writing before grading it. They must learn the importance of letting student writers know that their messages have been received and then of using that response, primarily through questions about content, to guide any revision those writers should make.

Readings

Mary Beaven. "Individualized Goal Setting, Self-Evaluation, and Peer Evaluation." In *Evaluating Writing: Describing, Measuring, Judging*, ed. Charles R. Cooper and Lee Odell. Urbana, Ill.: National Council of Teachers of English, 1977.

Charles R. Cooper. "Holistic Evaluation of Writing." In *Evaluating Writing*.

Muriel Harris. "The Overgraded Paper: Another Case of More Is Less." In *How to Handle the Paper Load*, ed. Gene Stanford. Urbana, Ill.: National Council of Teachers of English, 1979.

R. Baird Shuman. "How to Grade Student Writing." In *How to Handle the Paper Load*.

Pam Waterbury. "The Red Pencil Blues." *The Inkwell* 14 (1976).

Journal Assignments

1. Describe the best and worst experiences you have had with a teacher's response to or evaluation of your writing. What was the nature of the response or evaluation? How helpful or unhelpful was it? From your response here, develop a rationale for responding to and evaluating student writing.
2. Respond to assigned readings.

In-Class Activities

1. In peer groups, have students respond to and evaluate sample student papers. Groups should write a terminal comment for each paper and justify both the response to and evaluation of each paper.
2. Teach holistic scoring, using sample papers collected from various freshman composition classes.

Formal Writing Assignment

Outline your rationale for responding to and evaluating student writing. Respond to and evaluate two essays (either from your own class or provided by the instructor), justifying each in light of your rationale for response and evaluation.

Error

While it may be discussed in the context of response versus evaluation, error in student writing is important enough a topic to warrant separate treatment, because writing apprehension most often stems from the fear of being incorrect. Teachers with little or no experience in commenting substantively on student writing find errors in grammar and mechanics quantifiable and easy to mark. But in order to respond to the writer whose "sister was hit by a terck yesterday," the teacher must learn to look past the spelling error to consider the content first.

New teachers need to understand that the way they perceive error in student writing will help determine how they respond to that writing. To see problems in grammar and mechanics as the final, most important measure of writing is to limit severely, if not to destroy totally, the value of writing for the student. This is not to say that grammar and mechanics are unimportant; surely they are. But they should not be seen as the most important aspect of writing well.

Instructors should learn to do error analyses and should be aware of the view of error expressed by Mina Shaughnessy in *Errors and Expectations*. In this work, Shaughnessy points readers toward a new way of thinking about error, and her findings have helped many teachers find ways of coping with seemingly limitless error in student writing. One passage of her work is particularly representative. In it, Shaughnessy analyzes a paragraph of some eighty-nine words and finds thirteen that are wrong. Of the thirteen, however, ten are attributable to the same mistake, two to another, and one to another. So the number of errors at work in the paragraph is not thirteen but three. Rather than seeing a paragraph bleeding in red ink off the page, the student sees something manageable—three errors instead of thirteen.[17]

Readings

James L. Collins. "Dialect Variation and Writing: One Problem at a Time." *English Journal* 68, no. 8 (Nov. 1979): 48–51.

Sarah D'Eloia. "Teaching Standard Written English." *Journal of Basic Writing* 1, no. 1 (Spring 1975): 5–13.

Betty Rizzo and Santiago Villafane. "Spanish Language Influences on Written English." *Journal of Basic Writing* 1, no. 1 (Spring 1975): 62–71.

Mina P. Shaughnessy. *Errors and Expectations: A Guide for the Teacher of Basic Writing*. New York: Oxford Univ. Press, 1977.

Journal Assignments

1. Of what importance are grammar and mechanics in writing? In the teaching of writing? Why and how should we teach grammar and mechanics?
2. Respond to assigned readings.

In-Class Activities

1. From response to readings, develop a consensus on how to teach grammar and mechanics in the context of a writing class.

2. Using peer groups, have students do an error analysis for each of several papers, with Shaughnessy's text as a guide. Have them suggest ways of remedying any problems they find.

3. Using peer groups, have students develop individualized goal-setting procedures, with Beaven's essay as a guide. (See the preceding section's readings.) Have them suggest ways of remedying any problems they find.

Formal Writing Assignments

1. Outline your rationale for error analysis. Then analyze a student essay and outline a strategy for dealing with the problems you find in it. (Note: The essay to be analyzed may come either from the novice teacher's own writing class or may be provided by the training course instructor.)

2. Develop several strategies for teaching grammar and mechanics in a writing class. Use one or two of these strategies in your own class. Describe what you did and why. How successful was it? If you were to use these strategies in your class again, what would you change about them? Why?

The course outlined here is nothing if not rigorous. It involves a great deal of reading and writing, but the rigor is not a quantity-for-quantity's-sake kind of rigor. The readings, activities, and writing assignments are designed to engage the new teachers in the course, to challenge them, so that they examine their individual approaches to writing and teaching writing. The benefits of such a training course can be substantial. By considering the best of current writing theory and research, novice teachers can gain new insight into what it means to be a writer and a writing teacher and so develop increased or renewed respect for writing and the composition class. Such development can, in turn, begin to redefine the basics and so break the "schoolmarm" mold. Most important is the potential transfer of what new teachers learn into their individual classrooms. If inexperienced teachers come to value writing as more than mechanical skill, then they can provide their own students with a positive experience in a writing class. And when freshman composition students have a good experience in a writing course, they will be more inclined to take additional English courses, both in writing and literature.

Those of us responsible for training new writing teachers must help them become more informed about a subject vital to an English department's survival. Our job is to help redefine the basics so that inexperienced teachers see student writers and their individual writing processes as the focal point—the true basic—of any course those teachers present. If we can create a climate in which those attitudes toward writing that should be changed can in fact be changed by such redefinition, then we can help revitalize rhetoric so that it is no longer the "dreariest and least profitable part of the waste that the unfortunate travel through in Freshman English."

Writing is too important a means of learning to be dismissed simply as grammatical and mechanical skill. It can be an exciting and indeed profitable activity for student and teacher alike, especially when we view the writing course as crucial because it provides the tools for effective learning across the curriculum. We must work to help students and instructors alike come to value writing in a comprehensive sense. The logical place to begin such work is in a training program for new teachers that is solidly grounded in theory and research and that encourages new teachers to develop and implement a student-centered writing curriculum.

Notes

1. I. A. Richards, *The Philosophy of Rhetoric* (1936; rpt. New York: Oxford Univ. Press, 1971), 3.

2. H. L. Mencken, *The American Language: An Inquiry into the Development of the English Language* (New York: Knopf, 1936), 327.

3. Richards, 3.

4. D. Gordon Rohman and Albert O. Wlecke, *Pre-Writing: The Construction and Application of Models for Concept Formation in Writing* (Cooperative Research Program of the Office of Education, U. S. Department of Health, Education, and Welfare, Project No. 2174, 1964). For a summary of this project, see D. Gordon Rohman's "Pre-Writing: The Stage of Discovery in the Writing Process," *College Composition and Communication* 16, no. 3 (Oct. 1965): 106–12.

5. Francis Christensen and Bonniejean Christensen, "A Generative Rhetoric of the Sentence" and "A Generative Rhetoric of the Paragraph," *Notes toward a New Rhetoric: New Essays for Teachers* (New York: Harper & Row, 1967).

6. Richard E. Young, Alton L. Becker, and Kenneth L. Pike, *Rhetoric: Discovery and Change* (New York: Harcourt Brace Jovanovich, 1970).

7. See Robert W. Blake, "How to Talk to a Writer, or Forward to Fundamentals in Teaching Writing," *English Journal* 65, no. 8 (Nov. 1976): 49–55; R. D. Walshe, "What's Basic to Teaching Writing?" *English Journal* 68, no. 9 (Dec. 1979): 51–56; Charles Weingartner, "Getting to Some Basics That the Back-to-Basics Movement Doesn't Get To," *English Journal* 66, no. 7 (Oct. 1977): 39–44; and "What Are the 'Basics' in English?" *SLATE* (Aug. 1976).

8. Wayne Booth, "The Rhetorical Stance," in *Contemporary Rhetoric: A Conceptual Background with Readings*, ed. W. Ross Winterowd (New York: Harcourt Brace Jovanovich, 1975), 75.

9. James M. McCrimmon, "Writing as a Way of Knowing," in *Rhetoric and Composition: A Sourcebook for Teachers*, ed. Richard L. Graves (Rochelle Park, N.J.: Hayden, 1976), 3.

10. Donald M. Murray, "Writing as Process: How Writing Finds Its Own Meaning," in *Eight Approaches to Teaching Composition,* ed. Timothy R. Donovan and Ben W. McClelland (Urbana, Ill.: National Council of Teachers of English, 1980), 7.

11. James Britton, *Language and Learning* (New York: Penguin, 1970), 14.

12. James Berlin, "Contemporary Composition: The Major Pedagogical Theories," *College English* 44, no. 8 (Dec. 1982): 776.

13. For a fully developed essay on the topic of theory and research into practice, see Richard C. Gebhardt's "Balancing Theory with Practice in the Training of Writing Teachers," *College Composition and Communication* 28, no. 2 (May 1977): 134–40.

14. See Charles W. Bridges, "A First Day Writing Assignment," *FERN* 5, no. 2 (Spring/Summer 1981): 12–13.

15. For discussion and examples of an assignment sequence, see James Moffett, *Teaching the Universe of Discourse* (Boston: Houghton Mifflin, 1968) and *Active Voice* (Montclair, N.J.: Boynton/Cook, 1981).

16. Donald H. Graves, *Balance the Basics: Let Them Write* (New York: Ford Foundation, 1978), 7.

17. Mina P. Shaughnessy, *Errors and Expectations: A Guide for the Teacher of Basic Writing* (New York: Oxford Univ. Press, 1977), 117–18. In "Individualized Goal Setting, Self-Evaluation, and Peer Evaluation," Mary Beaven implicitly supports Shaughnessy's thinking here, suggesting that teachers not read for every error but only for the one or two errors troubling the individual student most. See Beaven's essay in *Evaluating Writing: Describing, Measuring, Judging*, ed. Charles R. Cooper and Lee Odell (Urbana, Ill.: National Council of Teachers of English, 1977), 135–56.

TA Training: A Period of Discovery

William F. Irmscher
University of Washington

Although the training of teachers of writing in university assistantship programs undoubtedly varies throughout the country, all of these programs ought to take into account two basic questions: (1) How can a TA training program be reconciled with an effective writing program? and (2) What is the role of the director in creating the proper climate for learning by students and teaching assistants alike?

For years freshman writing programs have been criticized for subjecting new students to inexperienced teachers after those students in their senior year of high school have probably been taught by seasoned veterans. The implicit criticism is that the college instruction is inferior, that young assistants could not possibly do as good a job as more experienced teachers, either those in high school or in the college department. That, of course, is a dubious assumption.

Freshman English classes do have one major disadvantage when they are compared with most other beginning college offerings. They represent the continuation of a long series of required classes in English; they are not the beginning of something new. Yet students characteristically expect the college experience to be something new nonetheless. Can freshman English be different if it is just more reading and writing? Obviously, it can be in terms of the selection of things to be read and the challenge of topics to be assigned. But curriculum is not the topic here. Teachers are. Teaching assistants, if properly trained, can bring new vitality to the study of English.

The New Teacher

Almost without exception, teaching assistants I have known (and I now have a roster accumulated over a period of twenty-eight years) approach their duties with enthusiasm. With fear and trembling, too, but with the

27

same kind of anxiety that characterizes any bold adventure. In their high expectations of this new venture and in their vulnerability, they are not unlike the students whom they will be teaching. They are both pursuing higher levels of learning—the students at the freshman level, the TAs at the graduate level. I never discourage TAs from telling students exactly who they are and what their status is. Students and TAs are engaged in a common enterprise of learning, and that can be an important bond of identification. They live in the same world; they do their work in the same places. Students frequently do not see regular faculty members in the same way. Professors somehow live in a different world of learning, seemingly more remote, more theoretical, more specialized, more settled. Needless to say, many of these perceptions are wrong, but students' perception of a gap between themselves and their more established teachers is not. Teaching assistants, then, by their youthfulness and relative inexperience paradoxically have a built-in advantage, unless they deliberately adopt mannerisms and strategies that sever the natural working relationship they have with students. Freshman students are more willing to write for someone who is likely to accept their ideas and values because no matter how bad their writing is, students characteristically attribute low grades to some fundamental disagreement between them and the teacher about content.

Despite the identification that arises from a bond of youthfulness, teaching assistants, ironically, are not always as disposed to open-mindedness as more experienced teachers are. Nor are they as tolerant of poorer work or incompetence. They are often shocked by the first papers they get. They need to be thoroughly cautioned to treat those themes gently. To destroy the first papers in an effort to prove that high standards are the new order is only to sidetrack the whole venture from the very beginning. It is difficult at a later time to bridge the rift that an indiscreet handling of first papers can cause.

"Anxious" is the exact word to describe first-year TAs as they approach teaching, even if they have had experience teaching things other than writing. We are asking them to do something they know very little about. Most of them are able and experienced writers, although they may have had no formal writing instruction at the college level, many having been exempted from the college writing requirement. They draw on their intuitive resources for writing and on their critical judgment derived from reading, but they have seldom had to verbalize how they do what they do or why they respond to writing as they do. The first thing a director must do is assure TAs that they know much more about writing than they think they do. Orientation should bring to a level of conscious awareness many of the assumptions on which they operate. It should also provide a coherent scheme for thinking about teaching.

Kenneth Burke's pentad works wonderfully well as a means of organizing all of the major considerations regarding writing and the teaching of writing into a plan for an orientation program. In brief, Burke says that anything involving motive can be thought of as if it were a drama, including actions, actor/agents, a scene (time and place), means, and purpose. The introductory orientation for teachers of writing can conveniently treat the actors, purpose, and scene: who is involved, why, where, and when. The act of teaching (action) and methods of going about it (means), on the other hand, require continuing attention throughout the school year.

Orientation

The three-day orientation program session for new TAs that we have before classes begin opens with a description of the University of Washington and a profile of our student body. Significantly, our average freshman student has a GPA from high school of 3.4 on a 4.0 scale, though despite this select quality, most students still come to the university unpracticed in writing. Given the opportunity to write and revise, however, they learn fast, bringing into play resources they have developed as superior students. Obviously, this is a situation different from that in many other colleges. TAs need to know not only that they have to adjust their attitudes and strategies to this particular student body, but, moving on at a later stage to other places, that they have to assess what conditions exist there.

Further, in our setting, we treat TAs as regular instructors, responsible for preparing their classes, reading student papers, and giving grades. This, too, is a different attitude from that found in many schools. Yet defining expectations makes clear what TA responsibilities are.

In his discussion of actor/agents, Burke points out that every agent may have coagents or counteragents. This point is useful in defining teacher-student relationships. Many students look on teachers as counteragents, as enemies, particularly if they do little more than find fault with student writing. TAs do not always realize that they need to think of themselves, together with students, as coagents working to overcome the common enemies of incommunicability and confusion of expression.

Seeking coherence in thought and expression is one of the main purposes of writing. Most TAs, not having thought consciously of their writing as one of their own most significant means of learning, characteristically talk about communication when they are asked why we should bother to teach writing. Communication as the prime motive for learning to write or teaching writing can be seriously questioned, and students often do. Technology makes it easier and easier to avoid writing. The point needs to be made that means of oral communication simply do not place upon the sender the same demands for structure, accuracy, and style that writing does. At any rate, an orientation program should help TAs think through why they are being called on to do what they are doing. Superficial objectives produce superficial programs.

What is the act of teaching composition? What does a teacher of writing say and do? Classroom strategies constitute, of course, one of the major concerns of anyone teaching composition. Many instructors are competent readers of student papers, but they have strong reservations about what to do with class time. They fall back on the cliché that composition is do-able but not teachable. They deny or ignore a body of recent research that can inform both teachers and students about the complex form of behavior that writing represents. If writing were only a skill, we would certainly have been remiss not to have come up with a simple way of teaching it by now.

Our preliminary three-day orientation session can begin only in a limited way to deal with the act of teaching itself. Orientation in some form or other has to continue throughout the first year. In these terms, TA training takes on two dimensions: (1) training for the immediate task of teaching courses to which assistants are assigned, and (2) preparation for the academic environment in which many of them will find their future occupation. Thus our preliminary orientation serves mainly to offer assurance to a group of concerned novices and to familiarize them with the two matters that will most affect their experience as teachers of writing: making assignments and evaluating writing. The continuing concern with day-to-day classroom practices has to be treated in other ways.

The eighteen hours of our orientation sessions are divided equally between large-group sessions and small-group discussions, each led by an experienced teacher. The TAs have assignments in advance. They compose theme topics. They comment on student papers. They prepare a lesson on an assigned topic. They respond to one another's work and generally begin to face some of the typical questions that they will need to answer as teachers.

Responding to Student Writing

Since students usually consider evaluating and grading among the most important things a TA does, and since appropriate comments on papers are one of the most helpful things a writing teacher does, we place strong emphasis during orientation on responding to student writing. At the end of the three-day sessions, each TA receives a student theme to comment on and grade as if it were the first writing assignment submitted by a student. Two assistants who work with me read the comments and write a brief critique of each evaluation, emphasizing matters of tone. The student's first response to the instructor's comments is all too often a lasting one. We therefore try to encourage instructors to learn how to make appropriate responses before their future students have even submitted their first papers.

After students have written their second themes, the instructor has evaluated them, and the themes have been revised, we ask TAs to submit an entire set of papers for review. My two assistants on this occasion examine the work in detail, hold conferences with the TAs to discuss the results, and write a summary report for me. This careful review is clearly one of the most important and helpful parts of our continuing orientation program. I have had teachers returning to school for an advanced degree with as much as ten years' experience tell me that no one had ever looked at their work. Yet they discover important things about themselves when someone else carefully examines their ways of evaluating student papers.

After looking at a TA's responses to student papers, we sometimes have to tell some that they are doing too much. They are overwhelming the students, and they are also burdening themselves unduly by spending too much time on each paper. Some people have to be encouraged to try selective emphasis—a kind of primary-trait analysis when students have been told in advance what the major emphasis will be. All composition teachers have to learn that every detail of every paper need not be scrutinized. Such an approach only reinforces the typical attitude of students that nothing they do can fully satisfy an English teacher. During the orientation sessions, I repeatedly quote William Stafford's wise words, which for me have become a kind of gospel: "In matters of writing, we must forgive each other much."

All our new TAs teach the same course. During the orientation, they receive a general syllabus for that course setting forth the objectives, requirements, and an overall teaching plan for the entire quarter. On each Tuesday of the first quarter, TAs receive a supplementary syllabus, discussing the topic for that week, summarizing recent research, sug-

gesting a number of teaching approaches, and always providing a list of
theme topics that TAs themselves have prepared during the introductory sessions. The syllabi may run from eight to ten typewritten pages,
single-spaced. They are not prescriptive in the sense that they direct
everyone to be on pages 59–63 on a particular Wednesday, but they do
expect everyone to be teaching the same topic for the week, perhaps
prewriting, paragraphing, or sentence variety. The syllabi provide background and resources. TAs are still left with the challenging task of
planning what will happen during each fifty-minute class session. One
of the fundamental premises of our training program is that individuals
must be able to discover their own talents for teaching. Like writing itself, teaching is a practice. There is no satisfactory way to learn about it
in the abstract. Even observing, helpful as that may be, is different from
practicing. How does one learn when to be flexible and when to provide
discipline, for instance? Inexperienced teachers can be cautioned about
obvious pitfalls. Beyond that, they have to have the freedom to fail as
well as to succeed and to realize that a failure this week is not a major
disaster, as long as one is willing to acknowledge that something did not
work and to try something different next time, or the same thing in a
more fully thought-out way.

I encourage TAs to talk with me and my assistants about teaching
and to discuss problems with their officemates. We pair new TAs with
experienced ones. This plan demands rotating offices at the end of each
year, but the effort is worthwhile in encouraging informal exhanges on
a daily basis.

For those who are uncertain how to plan class sessions, we also keep
resource files in the freshman English office, indexed by topics such as
voice, diction, mechanics, and heuristics. These files include dittos and
descriptions of lesson plans that others have found useful. They are
available for cribbing.

Our training program is not as sink-or-swim as this description may
suggest. It is an approach that provides some preliminary instruction in
the fundamental skills of teaching, then throws TAs in, each provided
with a life jacket and an assurance that someone is available to help if
he or she feels desperate. I understand why some of them go through
the first few weeks with trepidation, and why they think they need more
supervision than they actually get. But I have more trust in them than
they have in themselves. They learn quickly that certain things about
teaching cannot be taught; they have to learn by doing. TAs work hard
because they do not want to fail. They learn efficiency under pressure,
and their initial uncertainties diminish quickly. As full-fledged teachers,
TAs learn to respect what they do. In fact, in a graduate school setting

that too often forces them as students into passive, subservient roles, they derive emotional support from the activity of teaching.

Do TAs ever take advantage of this autonomy? Only rarely. I contend that no intelligent person likes to appear a fool before twenty-five other people, even if no superior is watching. A director cannot constantly supervise or intervene. Letters I have received through the years from individuals who have served as TAs in English refer repeatedly to their appreciation of the fundamental trust that was granted them at the same time that they were getting strong support. Training programs should not be planned in terms of possible abuses. They should be planned to make the best possible use of the intelligence and inventiveness of those who are teaching.

Observation

From the time I taught in junior high school many years ago and was prompted by my experienced colleagues always to have a "canned lesson" available for an unannounced visit by the principal, I have been skeptical about what one sees, either good or bad, on the occasion of a single visit, expected or not. From time to time, I have been asked by a TA to visit in order to diagnose why a class has not been going well. My response has always been that, if I visit, I will visit for a week, not a single day. In that period of time, I can usually make some assessment. Since I cannot visit everyone on that basis, I visit no one except on request, and everyone is considerably happier. But that does not mean that I do not know what goes on in the classes. One of the main sources of information is student surveys, designed especially for our writing courses and sufficiently open-ended to permit students to write their own thoughts. Through these, I have a fine sense not only of the classroom situation but also of the temperament and habits of the instructor.

In order to overcome the sense of isolation that can develop in a large teaching program, we conduct what we call a cooperative observation program, adapted from a program used at Indiana University under Michael Flanigan. During the fall quarter, new TAs are divided into pairs and asked to observe each other. In the winter quarter, new TAs are paired with more experienced assistants, and they observe each other.

The program, however, is more than visitation. It consists of three stages. The pair first meet for a pre-observation conference. They define for each other what they intend to accomplish during a class session and indicate any particular things they would like the other to observe. All observations are intended to be descriptive, not judgmental. What are the students doing or not doing? What is their attitude toward the teacher and of the teacher toward them? What kinds of questions are students asking? What kinds of questions is the instructor asking? TAs are provided a guide for class observation—what to look *at* and look *for.* They learn that observation is a skill in itself.

Following the observation period, the two again meet to discuss results and to talk about teaching in general. Then each writes a report to me, not evaluating the teaching of the other, but commenting on the value of the experience itself. Characteristically, most people say that observing is more valuable than being observed. That comment in itself may be defensive because almost all of the assistants reluctantly anticipate being observed and begrudge the time they have to devote to it. After it is over, the reactions are quite different. They unanimously agree that the experience is illuminating and productive. (I would add that I attribute their favorable response to the fact that they are being observed by their peers.) On being observed, two TAs made astute comments:

> Being observed was valuable for me because it gave me back my consciousness of what happens during a class period.

> I wondered if my rather fragile equilibrium would survive observation. But it did. In fact, weathering the observation process gave me more confidence in myself and my teaching.

Observation of others provides perspective—perspective on the range of possibilities in teaching and perspective on oneself, typified by comments like these:

> I am impressed how a good-spirited, nondirective woman can engage a somewhat lunatic class like this one. It reminds me how hard I have to fight myself not to be authoritative for the sheer hell of it, just because I know it is easier to do.

> This kind of revelation—that other TAs have to deal with the same problems I was facing in my own class—was, for me, the most important benefit of cooperative observation.

> Even more helpful was realizing I wasn't a failure just because I didn't have a perfect class every time.

> I learned a lot: that I have a lot to learn.

These are reassuring comments. They indicate the almost unreasonable expectations TAs set for themselves, contrary to the cynical motives some directors attribute to them. Observation tempers their demands on themselves, not in the sense that they compromise for less than their best efforts, but that they realize their best efforts may at times be misconceived or misdirected—failings of us all.

It is not possible to describe in detail other elements that are a part of our TA training program: videotapes, student surveys, grade-distribution reports, and voluntary meetings for those who want to share teaching experiences. The year's orientation culminates during spring quarter, when I have individual conferences with new TAs to review the year's work and to reflect on the teaching experience. These are usually honest and thoughtful exchanges that help me assess what commitment to teaching, especially to the teaching of writing, these individuals may have. They are conferences that give me continuing assurance that the training program works.

The Director's Role

What should be apparent from this description is that a major portion of a director's time must be concentrated on the TA training program itself if it is going to succeed. No one can teach full-time and direct the program as an overload. It is my opinion that good training programs are rare, chiefly because they are not adequately financed, in English as well as in other departments. Directing must be the prime responsibility of one professor, preferably a senior one. It cannot be something extra.

Training programs also suffer from transience among directors, another consequence of inadequate financing and of the attitude that directing can be done by almost anyone in the department. In fact, in some colleges, directing is even seen as a chore that everyone at some time or another ought to perform, regardless of his or her qualifications or interest. In still others, the job is seen as a stepping-stone to more lucrative administrative positions.

What a good training program needs is stability. It ought to have the continuing guidance of someone who considers the position a specialty. New rhetoric programs throughout the country are now training teachers who see themselves as specialists in writing and the teaching of writing. These are people who will bring professional status to composition, who will study and engage in research, who will publish, and who will bring to their work the kind of understanding and resourcefulness that the job demands. That kind of training and experience will also qualify specialists to direct new-teacher training programs, and give directors an ethos. That ethos is the same influence any good teacher ought to have on students. A director's attitude about the importance of writing will become the attitude of the assistants. They will learn the value of teaching writing. They will learn respect for what they are doing and not simply anticipate the time when they will graduate to what are too often considered the more significant areas of English studies.

TAs are student teachers, but they do not want to be thought of merely as apprentices. In fact, over a relatively short period of time, one can observe their growing cynicism about the lowly place they hold in the academic hierarchy. That too, unfortunately, is a foreshadowing of their forthcoming careers. Having reached the pinnacle that a Ph.D. represents to them, they once more start at the bottom professionally. That adjustment is likely to be easier if the training they have already received has prepared them to be self-sufficient and flexible teachers capable of adapting to varying academic situations. Only a training program that has helped them develop independence will adequately prepare them for the much greater autonomy they will exercise as regular faculty.

Linking Pedagogy to Purpose for Teaching Assistants in Basic Writing

Richard P. VanDeWeghe
University of Colorado at Denver

Perhaps the most pressing problem TAs face when starting their college teaching careers is "What am I going to *do* in my class?" Part of their training should therefore address this problem by providing them with numerous classroom approaches among which they can choose. But part should also emphasize that thoughtful teaching approaches exist in a context of theory and research. Those of us familiar with writing theory and research know the expertise that writing teachers with such knowledge bring to their classroom practices: they understand writing processes and the problems that beset writers at all levels of development; they analyze writers' needs and try to solve them in informed and systematic ways; and they develop and refine pedagogical approaches that, because they are derived from theoretical guides and research support, have an intellectual foundation that gives teachers sound reasons for choosing one approach or strategy over another.

TA training at the University of Colorado at Denver aims at linking pedagogy to purpose by helping TAs see how theory, research, and practice are interconnected. Though our TAs eventually teach at all three levels of the freshman composition program (English 101, a Basic Writing course; English 102, the general university expository writing course; and English 103, a research writing course), they begin with 101. So, my focus here will be on how they are trained to teach *Basic Writing*— as the course exists in the context of the entire program. Since the courses in our program are integrated in theory, research base, and pedagogy, TA training in Basic Writing has much carryover to other courses. The training consists of a presemester orientation and a series of vigorous staff workshops, the combination of which ensures that knowledge *about* writing connects with TA teaching experiences.

Presemester Orientation

At an August orientation meeting, TAs receive our booklet "Notes toward a Definition/Description of the Writing Program and Courses," explaining the theoretical and research foundations for our program. These are derived primarily from James Moffett's developmental theory,[1] James Britton's talking and writing theory,[2] Peter Elbow's writing process techniques,[3] Mina Shaughnessy's error analysis,[4] Donald Graves's process-conference model,[5] and the work of other researchers.[6] Since the classroom model is essentially a writing workshop in which students develop their writing in an active, process-oriented, collaborative setting, the concomitant teaching strategies suggested in the booklet include such approaches as free-writing; journal keeping; prewriting, writing, rewriting, and editing; peer collaborations; "showing writing" exercises;[7] and process conferences.

The booklet also describes each course in terms of its students and course goals, which further help TAs plan their courses. In this first instance, the following section from the booklet describes the students TAs can expect in their Basic Writing classes:

> Students enroll in the course because they perceive themselves as needing fundamental help with most aspects of writing, or because their writing has been identified through diagnostic testing as needing concentrated work in scribal fluency, basic sentence and paragraph structure, and a number of grammatical/mechanical areas. Most are writing apprehensives who have a history of failure in English classes and little experience as writers. Virtually all lack confidence as writers. Yet, once this confidence builds, they discover that they have rich experiences and insights about which to write in ways that will interest others (peers, teachers). They need to understand and master essentials of writing just to ensure their survival in the university. They need a realistic understanding of the composing processes available to them as writers. They need to understand prewriting, writing, rewriting, and editing as discrete yet reciprocal phases of composing. Also, they need to understand the similarities and differences between spoken and written language, and the power and situational appropriateness of each. They need constant and close guidance while logging a lot of time writing and while having someone respond to their writing in a supportive and instructive manner. Finally, they need the motivational context of "real writing"—which assumes an audience that responds to the content *and* mechanics of their writing. Most of these students find that working with a teacher who is genuinely interested in their ideas and the most successful transmission of those ideas comes as a novel yet welcome experience.

In the second instance, the booklet states these general course goals for Basic Writing:

  1. To reduce writing apprehension.

2. To develop student understanding of phases in and strategies for composing.
3. To promote student appreciation for the play, the beauty, and the power of language.
4. To develop student understanding and application of the rhetoric of the sentence, the paragraph, and the essay.
5. To develop student ability to use the usage forms and mechanics of edited American English.
6. To ensure that students' writing develops to at least the level of competency expected of them in English 102.

At this orientation meeting, we examine the writing program as a whole and the place of each course in it. We review the booklet—discussing, clarifying, and extending principles and practices. Thus, being familiar with the entire program and with their respective courses, knowing whom to expect in class, and having some broad goals to guide them gives individual TAs a vision of their work shared with other Basic Writing teachers, while also giving some unity to all three levels of the program.

The second handout at this meeting is a collection of articles addressing key practical issues: writing apprehension,[8] journal writing,[9] "rehearsals,"[10] collaborative writing groups,[11] writing processes,[12] assignment making,[13] and evaluating and responding to writing.[14] The readings provide additional insight into the program's rationale and describe many good teaching techniques, and since TAs read them in preparation for teaching, the readings extend our discussion beyond this orientation.

Though this meeting is all talk and thus still mostly theory for TAs, it remains an essential part of their training insofar as it provides both an intellectual and a practical introduction to teaching writing. TAs begin to sense the rich professional camaraderie they share with their colleagues, both here and elsewhere, in addressing teaching issues and problems. These TAs gain, in short, a far broader view of their coming work than if they were merely handed a list of disparate teaching techniques. This is particularly true of those teaching Basic Writing courses, in which the complexity of student writing problems and their solutions calls for a sophisticated understanding and humane application of theory, research, and suggested practices.

Staff Workshops

The second feature of our approach is a series of staff workshops held regularly during the school year. Part of the time in these workshops is spent on the interchange of problems encountered in teaching and group efforts at solving them, and part is spent in sharing effective teaching strategies. But the bulk of each workshop aims at developing further one of the key issues introduced in the orientation meeting. Over the course of a school year, we will consider in some depth such topics as writing apprehension, assignment making, collaborative writing groups, individual conferences, prewriting techniques, dialect influence on writing, and composing processes. Prior to each workshop, TAs prepare by rereading articles from the collection of readings and, in a number of ways, applying the information to their teaching. The intent of such combination of reading and application is for TAs to see the interrelationship of writing research and classroom practice, and thereby enrich their insight into teaching. The key here is for the workshop leader to devise some strategy whereby TAs apply or discover theoretical principles and research findings in their work with students. I will illustrate this approach with three sample workshops of most concern to TAs teaching Basic Writing, though these workshops are of much interest to those teaching other courses as well.

Workshop: Writing Apprehension

Preparation for this workshop begins at the start of the semester, when I ask TAs to have their students fill out the Daly-Miller 26-item measure of writing anxiety.[15] The data from this measure become a pretest of sorts with two uses: it gives TAs direct information regarding the individual students' apprehension, and, since the Daly-Miller questions have some redundancy (e.g., three questions concern evaluation, four concern audience), student responses often indicate whole-class trends. Therefore, TAs can use the results to structure their courses to meet both individual and large-group instructional objectives, such as reducing fear of evaluation, or reducing writers' blocks.

For example, Linda Vegh, a TA whose Basic Writing students filled out the measure, found that the majority of her students had little concept of other-than-teacher audiences and did not like the thought of others in class reading their writing. These results corroborated what Linda had read in studies of writing apprehension.[16] Accordingly, she used this information to establish teaching objectives to combat these sources of anxiety. She developed collaborative writing groups in her class more slowly than she had originally planned, starting with anonymous sharing of student writing at first and moving next to paired sharing and then to small groups of four or five students. This approach limited response and criticism at first, when the threat of "publication" loomed large, while it also built students' confidence in exposing their work to others. Linda also found that student fear of using incorrect grammar produced "getting started" and "organizing" blocks, that they had much fear of teacher evaluation, and that they had little confidence in their ability to do well in any composition class. She then incorporated specific strategies to meet these problems, such as Peter Elbow's thirteen methods for getting started called "loop writing,"[17] and the elimination of letter grades on papers.

Prior to our midsemester workshop on this topic, Linda had her students fill out the Daly-Miller measure again. She then compared these responses with the earlier ones, and was delighted with the results, for they showed that she was meeting her objectives of reducing apprehension: her students were enjoying having wider audiences read their work; writing blocks had been reduced, as had fear of evaluation; and the general level of writing anxiety had diminished. Linda's presentation of her findings at the workshop enriched our discussion of writing apprehension, for she was able to speak from recent and direct application of the research and was able to describe the benefits she and her students had derived from her applied research. The workshop thus crystallized the connections between the readings and actual classroom experiences.

Workshop: Assignment Making

TAs prepare for this workshop by rereading Eleanor M. Hoffman and John P. Schifsky's "Designing Writing Assignments" and Helen J. Throckmorton's "Do Your Writing Assignments Work?"[18] Each TA also chooses an assignment he or she feels meets the criteria for a good assignment as specified in either article; this assignment can be one he or she has used in class or would like to use. These assignments are duplicated in advance for others at the workshop.

I begin by passing out and reviewing the following statement, which serves as a theoretical guide for the workshop. It reiterates that part of the writing program rationale which argues that the "assignments" of real writers (professional writers, teachers) are the best models for student's assignments:[19]

What Do Real Writers Do?

They (i.e., people at certain levels of maturity and ability, with certain interests which may not be ours, with rich backgrounds and experiences, and with definite opinions of a variety of subjects) *write to someone* (a well-defined audience) *about something* (with which they are familiar) *for a purpose* (e.g., to express their feelings, to describe something, to persuade, to analyze) *in a certain way* (e.g., comparison-contrast structure, inductive/deductive development, formal/informal tone, reasoned/emotional, first person/third person point of view).

They Write to Someone about Something in a Certain Way for a Purpose.

In other words, each writing task a writer faces will differ, depending upon such specifications as those cited above. Yet in setting out to write, writers either know in advance or discover as they write the specifications of their assignment. It is knowing these specifications that enables them to write what they need to write.

Using real writers' assignments as our models, we review the criteria set forth in the two articles and then examine each sample assignment the TAs have prepared. Our framework for this analysis is simple: I ask, "What would Hoffman and Schifsky, or Throckmorton, say about how well this assignment meets their respective criteria?" This framework forces the TAs to examine the assignments strictly according to the criteria, and the subsequent analysis and discussion of assignments is lively, focused, and most instructive. TAs begin to see both the strengths and weaknesses of their assignments as we focus on the criteria met as well as those unmet, and then discuss how the assignment could be revised to include the unmet criteria. We find, for instance, the absence of the specified-audience criterion in such assignment questions as "What do you hope to explain to your reader?"—hardly a well-defined audience. Or, we find a clearly articulated purpose and audience, as in "Your purpose in this assignment is to capture the personality of the person you interviewed. After reading your interview, your classmates should know something about the character of the man or woman with whom you talked."

The entire process of preparing and critiquing assignments does precisely what a good learning experience should do: it produces change. Some TAs change their assignment-making practices by simply reading the articles; others change during the workshop as they begin to understand why an assignment is inadequate or why their students have trouble completing it. By focusing on the assignments' strengths as well as weaknesses, TAs connect the principles of good assignment making with their examples and, in doing so, firmly integrate the two.

Workshop: Peer Editing Groups

This final example concerns a workshop, also near midsemester, in which TAs examine the effectiveness of their students' collaborative writing/response groups. Preparation begins at midsemester, when TAs have their students respond to a course evaluation that includes a section for assessment of the use of writing groups in the course. TAs review student response to this section, looking for any trends in student opinion (good or bad) and any problems related to the approach. The intent here is to have the TAs collect the raw data and sort through the information to make sense of it themselves.

This assessment has many benefits. First, it gives TAs direct feedback on the effectiveness of writing-group approaches while they still have half the semester to change or refine them. Second, since TAs look for trends in the responses, they examine their data much as an applied researcher would—for generalizations that give insight and direction. Finally, because they bring their findings to our staff workshop, we can collectively examine the trends and problems they find, and connect these findings with the research that informs the writing-group model in the first place.

I begin the workshop by listing on the board and discussing some of the research on collaborative writing groups: the talk-write model of composing,[20] the importance of integrated language functions (speaking-listening-reading-writing) as they reinforce and support one another,[21] trial-error-feedback-reinforcement learning,[22] writing as an active human phenomenon,[23] the impact of immediate audience response,[24] and the growing critical independence writers develop through the writing-group approach. [25] Taking time to review the principles gives the rest of the meeting an integrative context, one in which the practical (their evaluation results) can more immediately relate to the theoretical (the research).

It works. TAs talk about the trends they see, the problems they need to solve (on which we collaborate), and how both are related to the research. None of this happens in any neat, mechanical way, for the discussion moves swiftly from findings to suspected problems to personal anecdotes to connections with research, sometimes all within a sentence or two. Often TAs talk their way to flashes of insight—"Aha" moments, the kinds in which we as educators most delight. I will share some examples.

At our most recent workshop on "Peer Writing Groups," one TA discussed the "biggest trend" in her Basic Writing students' evaluations: "They weren't getting enough honest response from one another," she said. "This seems part of the 'human' dimension of the model—that they need to be real with one another. This forced me to stop and say, 'How can I correct this?'" In our subsequent discussion of how this problem could be met, she remarked that perhaps she should talk with her students about how most of them wanted more honest comments on their work, though they felt reluctant to provide them. Opening up the issue with the class, she felt, would improve the quality of the students' responses. The workshop participants agreed and commented further that doing so would highlight the human dimension she wanted to emphasize.

Another teacher hit on both the interrelatedness of language functions and the growing independent critical judgment fostered by the group approach when she remarked, "It would be interesting, in the beginning of the semester, to establish *with* the students reading criteria for examining one another's work; then intermittently evaluate the criteria with them and see how they change, see *if* they become closer readers, more critical readers; and by the end of the semester, see if they have come any further. It would be interesting to see how their criteria change."

This growing independence was illustrated as another TA relished the fact that his students had reached a point through the writing-group approach where they would independently seek an audience for anything they wrote: "I had several students say that from now on anytime they wrote anything, they were going to get more of their friends to read it and comment on it. I knew then that the approach must have worked." I responded that, indeed, an ulterior goal of the approach is to have students no longer need teachers; hence the title of Peter Elbow's *Writing without Teachers*.[26] He continued by emphasizing the role of audience feedback in his students' development: "They just like the idea of getting feedback and having big holes checked out. They had learned that they needed to be more aware of the audience and they had become comfortable enough with feedback that they wanted it and were going after it on their own."

I have conducted many staff workshops of the sorts described above, and the results are always the same. Practice connects with research, insights spring from analysis and discussion, and TAs go back to their classes with a far richer understanding of their work than they had previously. Coupled with the initial orientation meeting, these workshops constitute our training program. TAs read about theory, research, and pedagogy, engage in situations where they collect data firsthand or manipulate their classroom materials, and participate in workshops in which the readings, data, materials, and classroom practices come together to enrich teaching experiences.

Notes

1. James Moffett, *Teaching the Universe of Discourse* (Boston: Houghton Mifflin, 1968).

2. James Britton, "Talking and Writing," in *Explorations in Children's Writing,* ed. Eldonna L. Evertts (Urbana, Ill.: National Council of Teachers of English, 1970), 21–32.

3. Peter Elbow, *Writing with Power* (New York: Oxford Univ. Press, 1981).

4. Mina P. Shaughnessy, *Errors and Expectations: A Guide for the Teacher of Basic Writing* (New York: Oxford Univ. Press, 1977).

5. Donald Graves, *Balance the Basics: Let Them Write* (New York: Ford Foundation, 1978).

6. *Eight Approaches to Teaching Composition,* ed. Timothy R. Donovan and Ben W. McClelland (Urbana, Ill.: National Council of Teachers of English, 1980); *Research on Composing: Points of Departure,* ed. Charles R. Cooper and Lee Odell (Urbana, Ill.: National Council of Teachers of English, 1978); and other research cited in subsequent notes here.

7. Rebekah Caplan and Catherine Keech, *Showing Writing: A Training Program to Help Students Be Specific* (Berkeley, Calif.: National Writing Project, 1982).

8. Lynn Bloom, "Myths and Mastery, Teaching Anxious Writers: Implications and Applications of Research," Conference on College Composition and Communication, Minneapolis, April, 1979; and J. A. Daly and M. D. Miller, "The Empirical Development of an Instrument to Measure Writing Apprehension," *Research in the Teaching of English* 9 (1975): 242–49.

9. Toby E. Fulwiler, "Journal Writing Across the Curriculum," in *How to Handle the Paper Load,* ed. Gene Stanford (Urbana, Ill.: National Council of Teachers of English, 1979).

10. "Rehearsals" are any pieces of writing that students regularly prepare in draft form for a small-group audience in class. The writing may originate anywhere, e.g., in a journal entry, a sketch made on the bus, a trial balloon for a class assignment, a letter. Time is allotted in class for students to read and respond to one another's rehearsals. Since the rehearsals are practice runs in which students experiment with ideas and styles, they are not graded.

11. James Moffett, "Learn to Write by Writing," in *Teaching the Universe of Discourse* (Boston: Houghton Mifflin, 1968); and James Moffett and Betty Jane Wagner, "The Writing Workshop," in *Student-Centered Language Arts and Reading, K–13,* 2d ed. (Boston: Houghton Mifflin, 1976).

12. Peter Elbow, "The Loop Writing Process," in *Writing with Power* (New York: Oxford Univ. Press, 1981); and Stephen N. Judy and Susan J. Judy, "Teaching the Composing Process—First Stages," in *An Introduction to the Teaching of Writing* (New York: John Wiley & Sons, 1981).

13. Eleanor M. Hoffman and John P. Schifsky, "Designing Writing Assignments," *English Journal* 66, no. 9 (Dec. 1977): 41–45; and Helen J. Throckmorton, "Do Your Writing Assignments Work?" *English Journal* 69, no. 8 (Nov. 1980): 56–59.

14. Mary H. Beaven, "Individualized Goal Setting, Self-Evaluation, and Peer Evaluation," in *Evaluating Writing,* ed. Charles R. Cooper and Lee Odell (Urbana, Ill.: National Council of Teachers of English, 1977), 135–56; David A. England, "Objectives for Our Own Composing Processes—When We Respond to Students," in *How to Handle the Paper Load;* and Elaine O. Lees, "Evaluating Student Writing," *College Composition and Communication* 30, no. 4 (Dec. 1979): 370–74.

15. Daly and Miller, "Empirical Development of an Instrument."

16. See note 8.

17. *Writing with Power,* 59–77.

18. See note 13.

19. This guide is heavily influenced by James Moffett's discourse theory in *Teaching the Universe of Discourse.*

20. See note 2.

21. *Exploring Speaking-Writing Relationships: Connections and Contrasts,* ed. Barry M. Kroll and Roberta J. Vann (Urbana, Ill.: National Council of Teachers of English, 1981); *Help for the Teacher of Written Composition,* ed. Sara W. Lundsteen (Urbana, Ill.: National Council of Teachers of English, 1979), 16–28; and Richard VanDeWeghe, "Research in Composition and the Design of Writing Programs," *ADE Bulletin,* no. 61 (May 1979): 29.

22. Moffett, "Learn to Write"; and Frank Smith, *Comprehension and Learning* (New York: Holt, Rinehart & Winston, 1975), 125–30.

23. See note 11.

24. Peter Elbow, *Writing with Power;* and *Writing without Teachers* (New York: Oxford Univ. Press, 1973), 48–116.

25. Carol Feiser Laque and Phyllis A. Sherwood, *A Laboratory Approach to Writing* (Urbana, Ill.: National Council of Teachers of English, 1977), 29–38; and Donald Murray, *A Writer Teaches Writing* (Boston: Houghton Mifflin, 1968), 129–33.

26. See note 24.

The Teaching Seminar: Writing Isn't Just Rhetoric

Nancy R. Comley
Queens College, City University of New York

Most universities with large freshman English programs staffed by graduate students require teachers new to the program to take a seminar in pedagogy. Traditionally, such seminars read and discuss composition theory and attend to such practical matters as evaluating student papers, preparing assignments, and so on. While such seminars are useful for new teachers of writing, helping them through their first teaching experience and laying the groundwork for further courses in rhetoric and research, they tend to ignore the needs of those who will not be specializing in rhetoric. With their singleminded emphasis on composition, they reinforce the existing split between writing and literature. What such seminars should do is to introduce theory and practice applicable to teaching writing not only in freshman composition but in other courses in the arts and sciences, showing teachers how to use writing as an integral part of their teaching. Such a course should make use of composition theory, literary theory, and creative writing techniques.

A Fragmented Profession

A training course integrating these three segments of the graduate curriculum would go far to bridge those notorious gaps that exist in English faculties among the literature people, the creative writing people, and the composition people, with the latter being the least respected group. Paula Johnson, Director of the Expository Writing Program at New York University, presents one reason for these gaps:

> Literary scholarship does not strive to effect anything, except maybe an advancement in academic rank for the scholars. Composition research, on the other hand, tries to do something to what it studies. The social analogue is plain: The leisured elite and the rude mechanicals.[1]

And from the literary side we hear Helen Vendler, in her presidential address to members of the Modern Language Association, deploring the public's lack of understanding of "what we do as scholars and critics." She includes what might be read as a challenge to composition people:

> The divorce of composition from the reading of powerful imaginative writing is our greatest barrier to creating an American public who understand what we love.[2]

Vendler's intent is noble in taking up "the question of how best to teach others to love what we have loved," and I am sympathetic; however, I wish she had suggested to her scholarly audience that they bestir themselves to learn how to teach writing with as much love and expertise as they devote to teaching literature. This is the real challenge to the profession: the task of changing deeply ingrained habits and prejudices.

When I started my graduate work in a department which then suffered from acute tripartition, I was led to believe that people who specialize in composition do so because they are neither bright enough to be literary critics and scholars nor imaginatively talented enough to be creative writers. I believed that composition was something that duller freshmen needed, and that because such students were boring to teach, they should be taught by duller graduate students. The brighter graduate students should be rewarded with sections of introductory literature courses. Of course, I was relieved and happy to be among those so rewarded. My attitude changed during my graduate career as I began to realize that many of my Ivy League students needed help with their writing, and as I discovered through work in creative writing and in the teaching of literature that it was possible to teach writing effectively and with pleasure. This moment of truth occurred at the end of an introductory poetry course in which students were writing responses to poetry, analyses of poems, and poetry itself. What struck me when evaluating the semester's work—which averaged eighty pages of writing per student—was not only that the students' comprehension of poetry had improved, but that their writing had also improved significantly without any comments from me on style or mechanics.

I now direct a freshman composition program, and I am regarded curiously by some, especially literature people who believe that no one chooses to teach writing to freshmen—they do it because they have to. Composition has gotten a bad reputation because it has been taught so badly by so many for so long. The worst of the composition people perpetuate this bad image. They are poorly read in literature, believing that behavioral theory holds the key to success in teaching writing, or counting tagmemes and making neat and meaningless charts, or searching for the Ur-sentence which, since it holds the key to all grammatical sentences, will allow them to plug Basic Writers into a computer and thus solve forever all those nasty remedial problems without human intervention. These people have no sense of the play of language, no idea that writing can be pleasurable, so determined are they that it should be prescriptive; and they usually write jargon themselves.

The other two English groups deserve criticism as well: the worst of the creative writers exist in little hothouse worlds hoping sprouts of deathless prose or poetry will poke their pale heads out and blossom into something publishable in a tiny journal with an odd name. They condescend to teach occasionally, and allow their adoring sycophants to be totally self-indulgent. You can spot the worst of their students at once: nothing they write is punctuated, and random thoughts ricochet across the page. Among the worst of the literary people are those who rely on an aesthetic approach ("Ah, there Shakespeare says it all!") or a my-explication-of-the-text approach ("What Yeats *really* means to say here . . ."). For both these types, the text is a beautiful artifact, a shrine to be worshiped, or a wonderful puzzle to be taken apart, piece by piece, and then restored to its exquisite unity before the students' adoring (or glazed) eyes.

And so, to graduate school come the products of some or all of these worsts: students who took dreadful courses in freshman composition taught out of grammar handbooks by people who hated teaching it; students who write poems but have never taken creative writing because those who did were considered kooks; students who are fairly adept at cranking out papers such as "Sounds of Music in Swinburne's *Atalanta in Calydon*." Today's graduate students have a better attitude toward composition than I had when I was a new graduate student. They know that in the present job market they must have experience in teaching writing. Yet I know that though they will undertake the teaching of freshman English willingly and even with enthusiasm, many really yearn for the day when they can teach a literature course and impress their dewy-eyed students with their One Right Reading of "The Love Song of J. Alfred Prufrock," just as their professors had done in those sophomore surveys of modern literature. Each year, nonetheless, there are a few more students who think of specializing in rhetoric. Often, these students are a little older, many of them having resumed their education after unsatisfactory experiences in secondary-school teaching, where they have found the curriculum they must teach too rigid. For them, the teaching of literature has been little more than a discussion of the plot and a quiz on the questions following the abridged selections in the anthology. The teaching of writing has consisted of long sieges with a grammar book and not much actual writing assigned because of the number of students they must teach.

I think they are all here because, like Helen Vendler, they too love the profession of English and still believe that the teaching of English should be pleasurable. They are right, and they are the people who can help the fractured English profession mend itself. Mending involves the acknowledgment that each segment of our profession has something to learn from the others, and that reading, analyzing, and writing have for years been wrongfully taught as separate skills. The most useful training for graduate students, then, should be a combination of theory and practice from composition, literature, and creative writing. An essential part of this training includes heightening the teacher's awareness and examination of herself or himself as reader and writer to better understand the processes of reading and writing. All texts—novels, essays, poems, or student papers—should be read as writing. Using a text effectively in a writing class means considering its process, the way in which it communicates to a reader, and how its structure determines the way it is read. The goal for new teachers should be a classroom in which both teacher and students actively read and write, and where reading and writing are the primary subjects of discussion.

The same principle holds true for the teaching seminar. The reading list does not have to be extensive; far more important are thorough discussions of issues raised in the readings and active writing both in and out of the seminar. I will limit my discussion here to a few texts I have found useful, and will provide other suggested readings in a bibliography.

Readers as Writers

Mina Shaughnessy's *Errors and Expectations* should be required reading for everyone teaching composition. It is especially useful in helping teachers discern and deal with patterns of error in basic student writing, where before they saw only what one colleague of mine described as "a word salad." But the book's usefulness is not limited to the teaching of Basic Writing. Teachers at any level need to be shown—or reminded— that student errors and awkwardness in writing result not primarily from sloppiness or ignorance but from the struggle to discover what they want to say. Putting little red handbook symbols in the margins of student papers is not a helpful way to guide students toward that discovery. Intervention in the process of composing and comments directed toward the writer's purpose are far more useful. For Shaughnessy, the process approach applies to the teaching of literature as well. She notes that traditional approaches to texts are "largely product- rather than process-oriented," with the text standing "outside, separated from the reader, impersonal and invulnerable, like some ancient tablet that the archeologist struggles to decode."[3] And how does the teacher appear? As keeper of the code, mantled in mysterious and powerful authority as she or he withholds the meaning—the One Right Reading—of the text, and interpretation becomes a classroom guessing game. While some students find this decoding approach interesting, most find it frustrating and not worth the effort to join what appears to them a secret society of privileged readers. And, as Shaughnessy points out, such alienation is detrimental to the student's development of reading and writing skills:

> This alienation of the student writer from the text robs him of important insights and sensitivities, for it is only when he can observe himself as a reader and imagine that a writer is behind the print of the page that he understands his own situation as a writer. (223)

What Shaughnessy suggests is "a writing approach to reading" in which "the *fact* of the reader's response" and "an effort to understand it, to discover what in the text or reader's experience created it" predominate:

> Reading in this way, the student begins to sense that the meaning of what he reads or writes resides not in the page nor in the reader but in the encounter between the two. This insight makes him a more careful writer and a more critical reader. As a writer, he must think about the kinds of responses his words are likely to arouse; as a reader, his growing critical stance encourages him to raise questions about what he reads, to infer the author's intent, and even to argue with him. And of course, these same critical skills can then be turned upon himself when he writes, for the purpose of writing utterly blurs the line that many college programs draw between reading and writing when they have two skills of literacy taught not simply in different courses but even in different departments. (223)

Shaughnessy's suggested approach not only makes good common sense, but is also the basis for much of contemporary literary theory, which is deeply engaged in such basic matters as what we do when we read, what writing is, and how writing differs from speech.

A background in such theory is useful for teachers of composition, who need to think seriously about their own processes of reading and writing before they can nurture the student's encounter with a text. For example, reader-response criticism is useful for working with students' subjective responses to texts and for a sense of what the act of reading is. For Robert Crosman, "reading *Paradise Lost*, or any text, is a process of making guesses, perceiving that some of these guesses are wrong, and then making improved guesses, which are in turn revised."[4] As Crosman describes it, the process of reading bears a strong resemblance to the composing process of experienced writers, with its recursive nature, dependence on the memory of what has been written, and awareness of the ways in which the written will affect what is to be written. And as experienced writers are those who have more awareness of audience than inexperienced writers, so do experienced readers have more awareness of themselves as collaborative audience in the process of reading.

Besides experience in reading, how well we collaborate depends on what we bring to the text emotionally and intellectually, and on the text itself. For, as Umberto Eco points out in *The Role of the Reader,* "a well-organized text on the one hand presupposes a model of competence coming, so to speak, from outside the text but on the other hand works to build up, by merely textual means, such a competence. . . . You cannot use the text as you want, but only as the text wants you to use it."[5] Building such a competence is the writer's role in this collaborative effort, and the text "cannot be described as a collaborative strategy if the role of its addressee (the reader, in the case of verbal texts) has not been envisaged at the moment of its generation *qua* text" (3). Eco's diagram and discussion of the interpretive movement between text and reader is especially useful because it attempts to categorize what it is we bring to a text and what mental movements we make in the process of reading. Eco's discussion is too complex to condense here, but let us take one area, that of the reader's competence, and consider two aspects of that area: the inferences readers can make in a text and the stores of common or intertextual knowledge, or "frames," as Eco terms them, that they draw on to do so.

It is logical to start a writing course with assignments that call on a student's frame of reference: that store of information which the student brings from daily life. Here, recall Shaughnessy's suggestion that the student be encouraged to understand his or her response to a text. The most common responses of inexperienced readers of literary texts are, "I couldn't relate to this story," or "I could relate to it." The next step is to ask students to say why—in writing. In the process of examining their subjective responses, students will read more carefully, and they will begin to find the text opening up for them. In their subjective responses, student writers may be very autobiographical; they may discover things about themselves they'd never realized before, or were never able to articulate before. The text provides a framework within which to write, taking the burden off the tender and undeveloped "I" of the inexperienced writer. After writing a subjective response, students are better prepared to look at the text again to see what the writer did to elicit their responses. Here is the beginning of critical reading, a skill that develops more rapidly after a student has produced a text which is the result of an active, productive reading of the original text. Writing assignments should be designed to help students enter into the text, to examine the choices the writer made, thereby learning how many choices they too have as writers. For example, they might take a Hemingway story such as "Hills Like White Elephants," which is presented mostly in dialogue, and retell it completely in narrative or from the point of view of a first-person observer of the scene. How is the story changed? How much have they learned about the characters from Hemingway's dialogue? From such an assignment, students can learn a good deal about narrative, a form of discourse not limited to fiction.

As students gain confidence in reading and writing, later assignments can be more analytical, and the development of intertextual knowledge in a more formal sense can begin. Drawing on intertextual knowledge means, as Eco puts it, that "every character (or situation) of a novel is immediately endowed with properties that the text does not directly manifest and that the reader has been 'programmed' to borrow from the treasury of intertextuality" (21). Such properties include literary topoi, narrative schemes, and rules of genre. Here is an area where the teacher must provide outside information because of students' limited intertextual information. For example, our response to John Crowe Ransom's "Bells for John Whiteside's Daughter" is further enriched when we read its seemingly unusual imagery through the generic frame of the Virgilian pastoral elegy, and can then see Ransom's lazy geese scuttling across Milton's high lawns. A less sophisticated approach is to present a group of twentieth-century elegies for dead children,[6] and let students discover the ways in which natural imagery is used. Ransom's geese will still stand out. It should also be noted that the students' own written responses to a text form a store of intertexts, and that the sharing of these responses in the classroom is an integral part of developing intertextual knowledge.

Literature in the Composition Class

Why use literary texts in a freshman composition course at all? Let us consider what James Moffett has said in *Teaching the Universe of Discourse*. Moffett, with his emphasis on the dialogue between writer and audience, suggests assignments based on a speaking-writing connection, the "very profound relationship that exists between literary and everyday discourse. . . . A student who writes a play is learning how to converse, to appreciate an art form, to understand himself, to describe, and, very generally, to write."[7] He further argues:

> Creating fictions, imaginatively combining real elements, is thinking. The fact that these elements may be characters, events, and objects does not make a literary construction less an act of thought than any other kind of abstraction. Art is simply a different *mode* of abstracting. It is a great mistake for the teacher to imagine an opposition between "creative" writing and idea writing. The ideas in plays and novels may not be named, as in exposition, but they are there. They are implicit in the selection, arrangement, and patterning of events and character. (111)

Semiotician Umberto Eco would agree. For him, not only does the fictional text provide "instances of every kind of speech act," it provides a fruitful area for learning how writing works:

> Certainly, narrative texts—especially fictional ones—are more complicated than many others and make the task of the semiotician harder. But they also make it more rewarding. That is why, probably, today one learns about textual machinery more from the researchers who dared to approach complex narrative texts than from those who limited themselves to analyzing short portions of everyday textuality. Maybe the latter have reached a higher degree of formalization, but the former have provided us with a higher degree of understanding. (12)

Along with that understanding of "textual machinery" come the rewards of working with the richness and complexity of the language of literary texts. And literary texts are, presumably, what graduate students in English are most familiar with, and thus the ones that they are able to teach with care and enthusiasm. But the same energy and the same writing approach can easily be transferred to the teaching of the referential discourse of disciplines other than English.

The goal is the same, no matter what the text: to enable students to "imagine that a writer is behind the print of the page," as Shaughnessy said, and to begin to understand what it means to write as a scientist, a historian, or an anthropologist. We should follow Moffett's suggestion that "a student writing in the same forms as the authors he reads can know literature from the inside in a way that few students ever do today. If the student has to work with language constantly in the functional way the professional does, he will come to know it in the professional's intimate way" (7). To learn referential writing from the inside, students should be provided with good examples of writing by scientists, historians, and anthropologists showing that writers in other disciplines take the same care with language that poets and novelists do. Discussion should center on the writer's purpose and the strategies used to carry it out. For example, in teaching that perennial favorite of freshman readers, the *Declaration of Independence,* one could spend a lot of classroom time discussing the structure and logic of deductive arguments. But it would be more useful to discuss Thomas Jefferson's purpose for writing, and why the structure of the deductive argument was appropriate for that purpose, and then ask students to write their own declarations of independence from some oppressive situation, using Jefferson as a model. Similarly, as they read Margaret Mead's "A Day in Samoa," students should be sent out to observe the inhabitants of a particular place, as Mead did, and write their versions ("A Day in . . . "), using Mead's essay as a model. In using this approach, students recreate the process that produces an anthropological essay, and they learn to write from the inside.

The Teaching Seminar

In the graduate teaching seminar, a writing approach should be used as well. It is crucial for teachers of writing to think of themselves as writers as well as teachers of writing, and the awful fact is that many new graduate students have done almost as little writing as the freshmen they are teaching. I mentioned above the classroom in which both teachers and students write together, and I repeat that suggestion here, because it is an important strategy in developing a classroom of differing personalities and abilities into a community of writers. Writing should be done in the seminar also, as an integral part of its curriculum. If Peter Elbow's *Writing without Teachers* is being read, everyone should free-write in the seminar. Graduate students can then experience the terrors, the writing blocks, and the excitement of discovery that their students experience—and understand better what it is to be an inexperienced freshman writer.

Another important writing requirement is to keep a journal of one's classroom experience, recording and reflecting on what went well and what did not in each class. Through the journal one comes to know oneself better as a teacher, and in the discipline of keeping a journal the teacher can experience what students experience when they are told to write and do not really feel like it. As part of the journal, I suggest that each teacher keep a record of the progress (or lack of it) of two of his or her students, noting the students' interaction with the class and the teacher as well as evaluating their written work. Such data can form the basis for a seminar paper presenting these case histories, augmenting journal observations with student conferences and with research done into special problems or strengths the students had as writers.

Another important seminar requirement is the creation, testing, and analysis of a writing assignment. In fulfilling this requirement, the new teacher must take into account the sequence of a semester's work (Where did we start, where are we going, and how fast are we moving?) and the needs of her or his students (In what areas do they need more practice?). Here is the opportunity to put seminar theory into practice, and to try out material one has always wanted to teach. Each seminar member must present a report telling what the assignment was meant to accomplish, how it was presented in the classroom, and what problems and pleasures were encountered by the teacher and the students during the process of writing. The teacher should provide her or his response to the assignment as well as a range of student responses for seminar discussion. This can be a humbling experience for the new teacher who finds that some of her or his students have produced much livelier papers than she or he has, either because the students were more imaginative or because the teacher suffered from the dreaded writing-for-the-(seminar) teacher syndrome. Such an experience is extremely valuable, even though it may be painful; more often, the new teacher finds that she or he knows what students need, and because she or he is enthusiastic about her or his presentation, the results are remarkably good. We learn more from our students about teaching than we learn from books. A poorly thought-out assignment produces poor papers—wise teachers know this, and unwise teachers must learn to face up to it, and abide by this rule: Never give an assignment you have not tried yourself.

The seminar is also a place to bring together members of the faculty from literary theory, creative writing, and composition to have them discuss their teaching techniques and theories of writing. No matter what our specialties, we all have much to learn from each other, and the seminar is a place where we can begin to bridge the gaps in our profession in fact and in deed.

Notes

1. "Writing Programs and the English Department," *Profession 80* (New York: Modern Language Association, 1980), 15.

2. Helen Vendler, "Presidential Address 1980," *PMLA* 96 (1981): 345.

3. Mina P. Shaughnessy, *Errors and Expectations: A Guide for the Teacher of Basic Writing* (New York: Oxford Univ. Press, 1977), 223.

4. Robert Crosman, *Reading Paradise Lost* (Bloomington: Indiana Univ. Press, 1980), 16.

5. Umberto Eco, *The Role of the Reader* (Bloomington: Indiana Univ. Press, 1979), 8–9.

6. Some other examples of modern elegies are Ransom's "Dead Boy," Theodore Roethke's "Elegy for Jane," and Dylan Thomas's "A Refusal to Mourn the Death, by Fire, of a Child in London."

7. James Moffett, *Teaching the Universe of Discourse* (Boston: Houghton Mifflin, 1968), 108.

Bibliography

This suggested bibliography is meant only to present a range of possible readings. Required reading for seminar members should also include such journals as *College Composition and Communication, College English, Freshman English News,* and *Journal of Advanced Composition.*

Barthes, Roland. *S/Z.* Trans. Richard Miller. New York: Hill & Wang, 1974.

Booth, Wayne C. *The Rhetoric of Fiction.* Chicago: Univ. of Chicago Press, 1961.

Eco, Umberto. *The Role of the Reader: Explorations in the Semiotics of Texts.* Bloomington: Indiana Univ. Press, 1979.

Elbow, Peter. *Writing without Teachers.* New York: Oxford Univ. Press, 1973.

Emig, Janet. *The Composing Processes of Twelfth Graders.* Urbana, Ill.: National Council of Teachers of English, 1971.

Fish, Stanley. *Is There a Text in This Class? The Authority of Interpretive Communities.* Cambridge: Harvard Univ. Press, 1980.

Iser, Wolfgang. *The Act of Reading: A Theory of Aesthetic Response.* Baltimore: Johns Hopkins Univ. Press, 1978.

Kinneavy, James L. *A Theory of Discourse: The Aims of Discourse.* New York: Norton, 1971.

Moffett, James. *Teaching the Universe of Discourse.* Boston: Houghton Mifflin, 1968.

Moran, Charles. "Teaching Writing/Teaching Literature." *College Composition and Communication* 32, no. 1 (Feb. 1981): 21–29.

Scholes, Robert. *Semiotics and Interpretation.* New Haven: Yale Univ. Press, 1982.

Shaughnessy, Mina P. *Errors and Expectations: A Guide for the Teacher of Basic Writing.* New York: Oxford Univ. Press, 1977.

Sommers, Nancy. "Responding to Student Writing." *College Composition and Communication* 33, no. 2 (May 1982): 148–56.

——— . "Revision Strategies of Student Writers and Experienced Adult Writers." *College Composition and Communication* 31, no. 4 (Dec. 1980): 378–88.

Suleiman, Susan R., and Inge Crosman, eds. *The Reader in the Text: Essays on Audience and Interpretation.* Princeton, N.J.: Princeton Univ. Press, 1980.

Tompkins, Jane P., ed. *Reader-Response Criticism: From Formalism to Post-Structuralism.* Baltimore: Johns Hopkins Univ. Press, 1980.

Fear and Loathing in the Classroom: Teaching Technical Writing for the First Time

Don R. Cox
University of Tennessee

First, some background information. When technical writing was first taught with any frequency on college campuses, about thirty-five years ago, it was taught not by English faculty but by engineers and scientists themselves. At a few universities today technical writing is still taught this way, usually by faculty hired and closely supervised by the engineering schools. With the rising interest in "high tech" careers generated in the seventies, however, many English departments found themselves venturing out, some for the very first time, on what seemed to be the very thin ice of technical writing. Several universities, mine included, went so far out onto this ice as to incorporate technical writing (sometimes euphemized into "occupational" or "professional" writing) into their freshman English programs, thus exposing dozens of new and often inexperienced teachers to the dangers of technical writing.

New teaching assistants in our program express a variety of emotions when they are told they will spend a part of their first year teaching technical writing—shock, fear, even anger. In fact, one assistant told me that he would finish his degree early, then resign his position so he would not face teaching technical writing in the spring. Such reactions may be extreme, but they should not be particularly surprising. Beneath this thin ice of technical writing lie the dark, threatening, and particularly murky waters of technology, filled with quasars, algorithms, and megabytes—definitely not a pool into which an English scholar would want to slip. Yet despite the technical language that can send shivers down the spine, the sometimes ominous and heavy-looking textbooks, and the prospect of confronting megabytes face-to-face in the classroom, the reality of technical writing is not nearly so threatening as the image it projects.

Although it has to some extent been shrouded in mystery—what one technical writer has called an aura of "black magic"—technical writing does not require special arcane knowledge.[1] It is most often practiced in what many technical writing teachers call the "real world" (as opposed, one assumes, to the "unreal world" of colleges and universities), by writers who did not necessarily choose it as their career. Although there are a few programs in the country that offer degrees in technical writing, most professional technical writers have no degrees in the discipline, or even much formal training in it. They are either writers— often English or journalism majors—with an interest in technology (or an interest in the jobs technology can provide), or they are technicians who can write. Technical writing is a kind of "borderline" profession that draws converts from both the sciences and the humanities. The fact that most technical writers, like Topsy, "just grew," should allay some of the fears of new teaching assistants who feel they must lay aside their training and (to speak technically) "retool." Retooling is not really necessary, but some rethinking is.

Stereotypes and Misperceptions

There are those who argue rather strongly that English teachers have no business teaching technical writing at all. J. C. Mathes, Dwight W. Stevenson, and Peter Klaver, highly respected teachers and writers in the field, recently contended in *Engineering Education* that engineering educators "must be wary of entrusting technical writing to English departments" because: (1) English departments primarily teach literature and will want to "water down" technical courses with more than a dash of the humanities; (2) the principles of technical writing are antithetical to the principles of traditional English composition; and (3) English teachers are primarily trained in literature and not in the teaching of writing anyway.[2] Because these objections come from respected authorities (who teach, we might note, in a college of engineering and not in an English department), and because their remarks reflect the criticism most commonly heard about English teachers teaching technical writing (and the questions teaching assistants most frequently raise), we might examine them more closely.

The first objection—that English departments primarily teach literature and the humanities—and the third objection (which seems to be only a variation of the first)—that English teachers are trained in literature and not writing—might have been true once upon a time, but anyone who has been involved in teaching English in this country during the last twenty years is aware that the rapidly increasing interest in technical writing by English teachers can probably be attributed primarily to their increasing interest in all types of writing. The fear expressed by Mathes, Stevenson, and Klaver that writing courses taught by English teachers are really only disguised literature courses reflects a prejudice based upon a misperception of what is really going on in English class-rooms today. But the misperception is common. A group of engineers involved in an accreditation review of our college of engineering visited my office recently. They came into the foreign territory of an English department to procure accurate estimates of how much time our fresh-man English courses spent on "pure English" (by which they seemed to mean grammar) and how much time was spent on "other things" (such as, I suppose, literature and the hazy humanities). Although they came seeking specific figures—"Would you say this course is 20 percent 'Eng-lish,' or would 30 percent be more accurate?"—they went away somewhat disappointed (and, I am certain, more convinced than ever that English departments were a hopeless case) when I tried to explain that our ac-tivities could not be quantified in such a fashion, and that teaching writ-ing was not at all the same as teaching grammar. It was quite clear to me throughout the interview that we were not speaking the same language, and equally clear that they were not aware there was more than one language to speak.

The misperception of those in engineering and the sciences may come from their own experiences with English courses before the fairly recent renaissance in writing took place. It is, however, no more intellec-tually irresponsible for them to judge us on their brief encounters with the humanities than it is for us to stereotype their activities—and we generally do. What would cause a teaching assistant to resign his posi-tion rather than teach technical writing if he were not reacting to the stereotype—the suspicion that technical writers must smell faintly of chemicals, or have a little grease under their fingernails, or carry sheaves of pencils in shiny pocket protectors, or have electronic calculators clipped to their belts?

Although the new teacher of technical writing might smile at the ste-reotypes that have been created on both sides, he or she should realize that a real temptation to succumb to the images fabricated by others exists, and that he or she should resist it. A technical writing classroom is not the place to teach "Bartleby the Scrivener" or "Rappaccini's Daughter," no matter how appropriate that might appear. There is, I might point out, some debate about how much "art" there is in technical writing. There are those who have identified "classics" of technical writ-ing—such as the writings of Vitruvius or the engineering documents of Herbert Hoover—and who have argued that there is more to good tech-nical writing than a utilitarian "scrub-brush" approach.[3] Even so, an examination of the literary or artistic merits of some technical writing probably belongs in its own "technical literature" course, and not in a writing course, where we already have more than enough to accomplish. It would be easy, if a new teacher were not careful, to make every engineering dean's darkest fears come true. But, if we keep clearly in mind the difference between a course in technical writing and a course in the humanities for scientists and engineers, just as we keep straight the difference between a course in English composition and a survey of American literature, we should have little problem defying the stereotype characterizing English teachers as merely translators of the mysteries of poetry.

In addition to the unconscious stereotyping of teachers and departments, there has been, I think, a certain amount of stereotyping of technical writing by some technical writing teachers themselves. Teaching technical writing, like teaching composition, has not traditionally been a job the profession has rewarded. If teaching composition has been regarded as one of the "dirtier jobs" in the department—and it has been until recent years—then the only thing "dirtier" has been technical writing. If composition teaching fell to only the disenfranchised—part-time instructors, teaching assistants, and departmental "deadwood"—then only the true outcasts, the untouchables, were given the opportunity to teach a course so antithetical to the department's primary goals. It is little wonder that the have-nots resented those in literature-oriented departments who gave them the least-wanted jobs of all. There are a certain number of articles on technical writing, in fact, that do little but sneer at those departments that have suddenly become interested in technical writing, something they had never previously cared about and never rewarded anyone for teaching. Perhaps because of this resentment among some technical writing teachers, perhaps because of a desire to protect a territory some had carefully staked out, perhaps because those who did not teach technical writing wanted an excuse not to do so—whatever the reasons, the legend then grew that technical writing was "special," was "different," was unlike other writing and required a knowledge of special "techniques," "strategies," and "style."

The generalization that technical writing is so different from other writing that, as Mathes, Stevenson, and Klaver argue in their remaining objection to English departments invading the field, "some of the principles taught in English composition are antithetical to basic principles of technical writing" (331–32) is, like most generalizations, only partly true. If we believe in and teach the principle of the five-paragraph theme, then that principle will have to be unlearned in a technical writing class (and in almost every other writing task most students will face outside of composition class). If, however, we believe in and teach the principle that writing should be clear, concise, and to the point, we have only assisted the technical writing student to become a better technical writer and have inculcated no "antithetical" principles.

John Walter, coauthor of one of the oldest (and largest-selling) textbooks in the field, examined the nature of technical writing several years ago in an article entitled "Technical Writing: Species or Genus?"[4] Walter concluded, and rightly so I think, that technical writing was simply a species of writing in general and not properly a genus (what a literary critic might label a separate genre). Obviously Walter's pronouncement has not been accepted as the final word, for the debate continues. Nevertheless, Walter's comparisons are very much worth reading and leave little doubt in my mind that there are far more similarities than differences between technical writing and "conventional" or "nontechnical" writing. The work of writing theorists and researchers that has taken place in the last twenty years—Kinneavy's hypothesis, with its identification of persuasive, expressive, and referential discourse, for example—only tends to confirm that teaching technical writing is not substantially different from teaching traditional composition, and this research weakens the claim that technical writing is something truly different and even unique.

The Job of Teaching Technical Writing

Now that we have examined some of the controversy over technical writing, let us look at the job of teaching it. Technical writing teachers, like composition teachers, differ in their approaches to teaching their courses. Since there have been fewer classes of technical writing taught than conventional composition classes, it is probably safe to assume that there are proportionally fewer approaches to technical writing, perhaps only a few thousand methods. Still, I will sketch out what seems to me to be the archetypal course—the one most teachers I have met seem to be teaching.

There is nearly always a term writing project, usually a research paper ranging from fifteen hundred to three thousand words in length, depending on whether the course is being taught in a quarter or semester system. Students generally begin the course by writing a proposal or prospectus for this term paper. That proposal is usually a formally graded assignment also. Then, while students are hurrying to the library doing their research (we hope), the basic elements they may need to incorporate into their final reports are covered—the abstract, cover letter, appendix—as well as certain techniques of technical writing, such as mechanism descriptions, process descriptions, and the use of graphics. Most teachers ask that these big reports be submitted several weeks before the end of the term so they can be graded and returned. Then, while the grading is going on and students have essentially finished the major portion of the course, student writers are often asked to give oral presentations on the subjects of their reports. Although these oral presentations are usually rationalized as being similar to "real world" presentations students may be asked to give later in life, I think the only real justification for them is to give the teacher a breather. I think they are a bad idea. The students are almost always extremely poor speakers and give terrible presentations; the students observing the "victims" are completely bored. It is far better, I think, to wind up the term doing something different, such as writing résumés, job applications, or business letters.

The chief fear teaching assistants have about teaching such a course—"I won't be able to grade the papers; I don't know anything about science"—is easily eliminated. One of the unique features of technical writing is that it is always addressed to a very specific audience. Because reports are "situational," that is, because they are written on demand, requested at a specific time in a specific context by an individual or agency, they are not like self-generated essays directed to whoever may stumble across them. Compare any piece of technical writing with the timelessness and generality of E. B. White's "Once More to the Lake" to see what I mean. A technical writer never sits down, as White presumably did, and says, "I think I'll write up an idea I had yesterday." His or her writing is temporal—one consults a service manual when repairs need to be made, not to pass the time on a rainy afternoon—and is created in response to a particular situation, usually at the request of others who are directing the research. And these are very important differences.

The teacher of a technical writing class begins by establishing the proper audience for the reports that will be written. There are several systems for identifying and classifying potential audiences, but all of them include the one important category *layperson*.[5] Here is where most teachers take refuge, and they are justified in doing so. In "conventional" writing—literary criticism for example—it is possible to read an article that is "over your head," too difficult to follow. We usually do not hold the critic responsible in these situations (although I suspect sometimes we should), but assume that we are not as knowledgeable as we might be. That is not the case in technical writing. Because the writer knows the context in which the report is written, and knows who its audience will be, if the reader does not understand the report the blame falls squarely on the shoulders of the writer. In short, if the student does his or her job correctly, it should be impossible for the teacher *not* to understand.

The real problem teaching assistants face stems from the textbooks themselves. Naturally, with dozens of new technical writing textbooks entering the marketplace each year, it is difficult to make a definitive pronouncement about the present state of all available texts. Still, teachers will find that the older texts (and in this rapidly expanding field, texts become "old" very quickly) tend to cling to what I have called the "black magic" approach, hiding behind the mystique of technical writing by maintaining that technical writing is something special and different. Texts using this approach tend to emphasize the uniqueness of technical writing, focusing on forms and formats—and little else. Some books, in fact, are only "format" books: "Here is the format for the proposal. Here is the format for the progress report," etc. New teaching assistants come back from their classes after using such texts contending (1) that there is nothing for them to teach because the format says it all, and (2) that the assignments are difficult to grade—everyone gets an A—because the students only need to "fill in the blanks" of the format. Rather than finding themselves struggling with a course that is far above their heads, many teaching assistants unexpectedly find themselves in a "non-course" that is simple to the point of boredom.

The problem here, however, is not that technical writing is too simple; it is that many of the textbooks used do not attack the essence of the course. First of all, almost every technical writing textbook available assumes that students are already competent writers. Anyone who has ever taught at the college level will immediately see the fallacy of that assumption. Teachers should remember that the students enrolled in technical writing courses are exactly those students who have repeatedly chosen science courses over those in the humanities and social sciences (where at least a medium amount of writing is sometimes required). In short, rather than assuming that technical writing students already know how to write, new instructors would do well to expect the reverse, remembering that their students are often bright but inexperienced. A fair amount of class time will need to be spent on fundamental writing issues, particularly on identifying audiences and tailoring prose to fit those audiences. Most texts seem to assume that form and content are separable in technical writing. Examination and discussion of the simple writer-reader-subject triangle (which is something that rarely appears in technical writing texts) would seem to be a necessary element of any technical writing course.

A second element of technical writing ignored by most texts usually gives students (and indirectly teachers) more headaches than anything else, and that is thinking, particularly problem solving. After students have selected a topic, compiled a mass of data, and created a decent proposal, they are usually given a format and told to "write it up." "Writing it up" is, of course, the main problem *any* writer, technical or otherwise, ever faces. Students, more often than not, will be unable to understand and assimilate the data they have assembled. They will not know what should go first, what should go second, and what should be thrown out. They will not know whether the solution they have arrived at is really a solution, or just an extension of the problem. They will be unable to separate causes from conclusions. The ability of students to resolve these problems will determine their success as technical writers and technical thinkers, although the difficulties the students will have in this respect will not always be visible to the teacher (who assumes that everything is going smoothly) until the end of the term, when students suddenly descend on his or her office in despair. At that point it is really too late to explain to anguished students that they cannot solve the problems their papers hope to, because they have never clearly identified those problems in the first place. Such times are not for a teaching assistant who is faint of heart.

New teachers who have been forewarned of such potential traumas (and you should now consider yourself forewarned, if you are one) should prepare for this eventuality early in the course. Some time must be set aside for the study of logic, for task analysis, and for exploring various heuristics, as well as for standard material such as induction and deduction. Those teachers who are really on the cutting edge may wish to explore cultural thought patterns, problems of conceptualization, and that which goes by the teasingly simple name *creativity*. A book such as James Adams's *Conceptual Blockbusting* (New York: Norton, 1980) will provide more material than any teacher can squeeze into a term, but time spent on such activities will profit both teacher and student when the term papers begin to stack up.

Next, a word about formats. The formats that textbooks present are somewhat like styles of documentation—no two, as they are presented in print, are exactly alike. That fact is sometimes shocking to students when they discover a highly prescriptive format for a feasibility study that differs substantially from the equally prescriptive format that appears in their textbooks. The differences in formats should not be tremendously important to teachers, because it is presumably the discipline of following a format, rather than the specifics of that format, that matters. Still, one wonders why some texts seem to indicate such specific and unalterable formats that each technical writing project is mostly a matter of putting the final pages in the proper arrangement.

Obviously I do not think that focusing heavily on formats is a very important activity. What is far more important, I think, is making students understand that *they* as writers will often select or create the proper format for their work. They will have to decide whether a proposal should be formal or informal, whether a feasibility study is needed, and whether a progress report will help alleviate the worries superiors are having about a project or just slow everything down that much more. To be sure, sometimes technical writers will be asked to "fill in the blanks" of a prescribed format, but even then it is the flexibility of the task that creates the problems. Most texts, for example, contain a chapter on graphics, and generally these chapters describe the various graphic aids available. But what these chapters on graphics usually do not make clear is that no employer will ever say "Give me a report with six graphic aids, one of which should be a pie chart." Students should understand that they themselves will be the ones who decide whether graphic aids should be used in their reports, what material, if so, should be represented graphically, and which types of graphic aids should be used. All these decisions will be affected by the reproduction facilities available to the writers. The use of graphic aids is another problem-solving activity; these aids should be seen as something that interacts with and reinforces a writer's prose, not as something independent from the content of a report that is simply dropped in as flavoring or decoration.

Finally, the emphasis on specific formats obscures the real functional nature of technical writing. Technical writing has been called "writing that works"; it is not writing that is "technical" because it obeys a series of prescribed formulae. Again, one of the central elements distinguishing technical writing from other prose is that it is situational, contextual. Approaching the subject through a format-oriented approach causes students to lose sight of the fact that their writing has a functional purpose, a reason for being. For these reasons new teaching assistants should be very careful about creating assignments that are "canned," because these assignments will not only produce writing that is dull and flat, they will also generate writing that has the form of technical writing but none of the functional quality that is its essence. For example, telling students to include in their term papers at least three graphic aids, or to use two footnotes per page, or to include ten items in their bibliographies (and these are all things I have seen new teachers do) smacks of phoniness. Even sending students to the library to find a topic is a blatantly artificial exercise. No technical writer is ever told to "find a topic."

In my experience, the best classes involve an assignment generated by the teacher, who serves as a kind of "chair of the board" of a fictional corporation. The teacher introduces a project with many facets—say the rehabilitation of an inner-city ghetto, the development of a new theme park, or, one of my favorites, the construction of the mile-high skyscraper for which Frank Lloyd Wright actually drew up the specifications.[6] The more complex the project, the more topics it will provide (the recent World's Fair, for example, generated hundreds of student papers at my university). Students can then be assigned problems roughly parallel to their own majors and interests—landscaping, electrical engineering, business and finance, etc. They will be forced to conceptualize, limit, organize, and actually solve their individual problems in reports that will be filed with the chair of their corporation—the teacher. The trick, of course, is to come up with the right project, but sometimes the students themselves can help dream up the master project that will generate all their work for the next few months. Such an approach should stress the functional nature of their writing, tax their problem-solving powers to the utmost, produce papers that are very interesting for the teacher to read, and, not least important, truly engage students in the activities of the class. They will *need* to know how to describe a mechanism, or write an abstract, in order to carry out their projects, and this need for information can change the atmosphere of a classroom tremendously. Understanding and then writing a paper on "My Last Duchess" may be necessary for passing an English class, but students do not always feel there is a real point to such exercises, and frequently attack them with less fervor than we would like. The advantage of a "real world" project like the one I have described is that its relevance is easily grasped by the average student in the class. Students become excited when they discover that there is something relevant—finally—about English.

In summary, I would suggest that new teaching assistants lay aside whatever prejudices and preconceptions they may have about teaching technical writing. It is a subject with its difficulties, but teaching writing of any kind always has difficulties; and the genuine relevance of technical writing is, I am convinced, the reason that almost all of our new teaching assistants, after having been required to teach the course the first time, elect to teach technical writing over and over. They very quickly overcome their initial fear and loathing.

Notes

1. Robert L. Corey, "Rhetoric and Technical Writing: Black Magic or Science?" *Technical Communication*, 1978, no. 4: 2–6.

2. J. C. Mathes, Dwight W. Stevenson, and Peter Klaver, "Technical Writing: The Engineering Educator's Responsibility," *Engineering Education* 69 (1979): 331–34.

3. See, for example, the bibliography accompanying a recent editorial in a leading computer magazine: Chris Morgan, "What's Wrong with Technical Writing Today?" *BYTE*, Dec. 1980, 6–12, 294.

4. John A. Walter, "Technical Writing: Species or Genus?" *Technical Communication*, 1977, no. 2: 6–8.

5. For the best discussion of audience see Thomas Pearsall, *Audience Analysis for Technical Writing* (Beverly Hills, Calif.: Glencoe Press, 1969).

6. See Frank Lloyd Wright, *A Testament* (New York: Bramhall House, 1957), 239–40.

The Literature Major as Teacher of Technical Writing: A Bibliographical Orientation

O. Jane Allen
New Mexico State University

As enrollment continues to increase in lower-division technical writing courses, English departments across the country are faced with staffing problems. Graduate students of literature have long been a valuable resource in staffing traditional freshman composition courses; they can be an equally valuable resource to departments who need additional faculty to teach lower-division technical writing courses. Many of these students have much to offer students in other disciplines. They are accomplished at research; they are skillful, analytical readers; they write well themselves; and their love of the language can motivate them to handle some of the special problems of style that face technical writing students.

Students of literature often, however, need some help in making the transition from the literature or freshman composition classroom into the technical writing classroom. We can help them by recommending texts and by providing clear, detailed course outlines to guide them through their first semesters in the technical writing classroom. Just as important, however, is the need to answer some of the questions many of them may ask: Just what *is* technical writing? How can I, without a technical background, teach it? Won't I find technical writing extremely dull compared to my work in literature? To answer these questions, we can begin by helping them place technical writing in a context with other kinds of writing, by helping them see that the analytical and writing skills they have developed as literature majors will serve them well in the technical writing classroom, and by showing them that technical writing offers interesting and challenging areas for research.

Defining Technical Writing

Particularly helpful in defining technical writing, because it helps one to see technical writing in context with other kinds of writing, is James

L. Kinneavy's discussion of referential discourse in *A Theory of Discourse* (New York: Norton, 1971). Kinneavy breaks the universe of discourse into four categories according to the aim of a particular discourse. Allowing that in all discourse the decoder or audience is the primary element, and that all modes of discourse overlap one with another, Kinneavy offers four categories: expressive, persuasive, literary, and referential. Expressive discourse, which has its focus on the encoder or originator, includes individual forms of discourse, such as diaries and prayer, and social forms, such as myths and manifestos. Persuasive discourse, which has its focus on the decoder, and in which the acceptance of the audience is directly solicited, includes advertising, political speeches, and editorials. Literary discourse, with its focus on the signal or discourse product, includes the short story, the lyric, the drama, and the joke. It is discourse that calls attention to itself "as an object of delight" (88). Finally, referential discourse, the category under which most technical writing would appear to fall, has its primary emphasis on "reality," on the subject matter to which reference is made.

Under referential or reality-oriented discourse, Kinneavy presents three subcategories: exploratory discourse, such as dialogues and seminars; scientific discourse, which proves a point inductively or deductively; and informative discourse, which includes news articles, reports, and textbooks. Viewed from Kinneavy's referential perspective, the "technical" in technical writing may be a misnomer. The uninitiated often assume that technical writing deals only with writing about such subjects as assembling electronic gear or stereo components. Yet much of the referential discourse we teach under the rubric of "technical writing" has little to do with describing technology. Students in technical writing courses are often involved in many of the types of writing Kinneavy classifies as referential discourse. And literature majors themselves have experience in reading and writing many of these types of writing. The expository papers they have written for composition and history and philosophy courses, and the analysis of literature that finds its way into their critical papers in English courses, have prepared them well to teach technical writing students to analyze a topic and organize a technical paper.

Also helpful in defining technical writing is a distinction drawn by Linda Flower in "Communication Strategy in Professional Writing: Teaching a Rhetorical Case" (in *Courses, Components, and Exercises in Technical Communication*, ed. Dwight W. Stevenson et al. [Urbana, Ill.: National Council of Teachers of English, 1981]). In this essay, Flower differentiates professional writing courses from other writing courses, noting that the foremost goal in professional writing is "to teach students to develop a communication strategy" (34), that is, to make a "self-conscious attempt . . . to get through to the reader—to communicate, not merely to express" (36). The professional writer—and she emphasizes that "professional writing is the writing all of us do after we leave school" (35)—needs to be able to integrate his or her purpose with the reader's need. In essence, Flower contrasts technical or professional writing with expressive writing by noting the former's focus on a reader—and on the need to communicate information to that reader. From this point of view, audience and communication receive primary emphasis in technical writing. This increased emphasis on audience, in conjunction with its emphasis on referential aims, is the primary distinction between technical writing and other kinds of writing.

Emphasis on Audience

Two essays by Thomas E. Pearsall can be especially helpful in defining for the teacher the elements of audience analysis. First, Pearsall's introductory essay to *Audience Analysis for Technical Writing*, ed. Pearsall (Beverly Hills, Calif.: Glencoe Press, 1969) emphasizes that students must learn to think not only about their own purposes but about the purposes of their audience—what, in fact, the reader will *do* with the information provided by the technical writer. Pearsall analyzes five different audiences: the lay audience that reads for interesting facts that add to awareness; the executive audience, whose motive may be profit; the expert audience that desires new information, information that might stimulate research; the technician audience that needs information in order to understand and maintain equipment; and the operator audience that needs operating instructions. His advice to teachers is to shift their perspective on writing so that it focuses on the audience's needs and purposes (ix-xxii). Then, in "The Communication Triangle" (in *Teaching Technical Writing: Teaching Audience Analysis and Adaptation*, ed. Paul V. Anderson [Miami, Ohio: Association of Teachers of Technical Writing, 1980]), Pearsall discusses audience, purpose, and message and provides a worksheet for helping students sort out these three elements of the "basic triangle of technical and occupational writing" (2).

In addition to the Pearsall essay, Anderson's anthology contains other essays that can help the novice teacher gain insight into teaching audience awareness. Myron L. White, in "The Informational Requirements of Writing," emphasizes that the audience determines not only the linguistic style of communication but also its content—how much the audience needs to know in order to perform a particular task. David L.

Carson, in "Audience in Technical Writing: The Need for Greater Realism in Identifying the Fictional Reader," comments on the functional demands of technical communication that require attention to audience. And Merrill D. Whitburn, in "Audience: A Foundation for Technical Writing Courses," suggests that teachers of technical writing teach audience analysis by practicing it themselves with their students and by adapting their courses to the specific needs of the students who take them. In this respect, Whitburn divides most technical writing students into three groups: (1) those who take technical writing courses to prepare them for communication tasks in such professions as engineering or accounting, (2) those who intend to become full-time professional communicators, and (3) graduate students who intend to teach or develop technical writing courses and conduct research in the field (18–19). Finally, for further reading, this anthology contains a bibliographical essay, "Audience Analysis for Technical Writing: A Selective, Annotated Bibliography," by Whitburn and Michael L. Keene.

Another essay offering helpful suggestions for teaching audience awareness is "Teaching Audience Analysis to the Technical Student" by M. B. Debs and L. V. Brillhart, in *Technical Communications: Perspectives for the Eighties,* Proceedings of the Thirty-second Conference on College Composition and Communication, ed. J. C. Mathes and T. E. Pinelli (Hampton, Va.: National Aeronautics and Space Administration, 1981). Debs and Brillhart write that in teaching audience analysis we need to go beyond a "cookbook" approach that merely identifies the audience and its level of expertise. We need to teach students to "internalize an audience, to adopt the role of the reader" (539) in order to help them develop awareness of the reader's frame of reference or disposition toward a subject. Debs and Brillhart suggest that assignments be labeled with a defined audience, that instructors respond to student writing in fictive roles, and that students themselves be required to assume the role of reader of other students' papers. They further suggest that, prior to writing a report, students be required to analyze their potential readers, including the attitudes of those readers compared to theirs as writers and the effect that sections of a report should have on an audience, and that they be required to make a case for a specific strategy or appeal. This emphasis on audience in the literature on technical writing reflects the attention audience analysis often receives in the technical writing classroom.

Emphasis on Visual Aids

Inherent in the emphasis on audience in the technical writing course is an emphasis on visual aids that helps differentiate technical writing from other kinds of writing. To enhance the readability and comprehensibility of a piece of writing, the technical communicator must consider the visual effect of that writing. This emphasis on visual aids includes such techniques as the use of white space on the page and of relatively short paragraphs to make the page inviting to the eye; the use of heads and subheads to guide a reader through a longer piece of writing; the use of lists and such graphic aids as bullets to set off their entries; the use of charts, tables, and graphs to present statistical information; and the use of drawings, photographs, and other illustrations to develop and complement the text or merely to rest the eye. Visual or graphic aids are important to both writer and audience in technical writing. As Robert Cury writes in "Visual/Graphic Aids for the Technical Report," *Journal of Technical Writing and Communication* 9, no. 3 (1979), they not only allow the writer to condense information on the page, but they make it psychologically easier for the reader to grasp information.

While graphics may be unfamiliar territory to the literature major, there are some helpful guides available. A. J. MacGregor's *Graphics Simplified: How to Plan and Prepare Effective Charts, Graphs, Illustrations, and Other Visual Aids* (Toronto: Toronto Univ. Press, 1979) offers a concise guide to planning and preparing visual aids. More extensive coverage can be found in Robert Lefferts's *How to Prepare Charts and Graphs for Effective Reports* (New York: Barnes & Noble, 1982). Lefferts offers step-by-step directions to the nonartist for preparing bar charts, pie charts, line charts, organization charts, flow charts, and time-line charts. His focus is on graphics that are "suitable for inclusion in typewritten reports and that can be reproduced using the various types of duplicating machines available to most organizations and offices" (2). One chapter of this text, "Principles of Graphics," applies the principles of unity, balance, contrast, and meaning to graphics presentations. Another chapter, "The Nine Uses of Graphics," offers suggestions for strategy in the use of graphics; and another chapter lists and describes the basic supplies needed to prepare the graphics Lefferts explains in his book.

Emphasis on Collaborative Work

The technical writing course, then, differs from other writing courses primarily in its increased emphasis on audience analysis, which in turn leads to increased emphasis on the use of visual aids. The emphasis on audience analysis also fosters an emphasis on purposeful, practical collaborative work. Collaborative work is important for two obvious reasons: Students learn from one another when they work together; and since they can expect to work in collaboration with others once they leave the nest of academia, working in groups in the technical writing course offers experience in an environment similar to the one they are likely to find in the professional world. Jone Rymer Goldstein has noted that in addition to encouraging students to learn from one another, group work offers students the opportunity to engage in authentic oral dialogue and to develop skills in such dialogue that will be important to both written and oral professional communication ("Integrating Oral Communication Skills into the Technical Writing Course," *Proceedings, Twenty-Seventh International Technical Communication Conference* [Washington, D.C.: Society for Technical Communication, 1980]). Gerald J. Gross, in "Group Projects in the Technical Writing Course" (in *Courses, Components, and Exercises in Technical Communication,* ed. Dwight W. Stevenson et al. [Urbana, Ill.: National Council of Teachers of English, 1981]), emphasizes the importance of group work in government and industry and writes that having students work in groups introduces them to problems of organization, style, and scheduling they might expect in the professional world, while it gives them a keener sense of audience—an awareness that they are communicating *with* someone.

Group work can take a number of forms. Students can be assigned to specific groups or encouraged to work in groups of two or three on a report assignment, or they can work individually to research and write a report and then work in groups to edit and revise the individually written reports. Both Goldstein and Gross offer suggestions for handling collaboration in the classroom. In addition, Linda K. Stout Chavarria, in "Using Workshop Sessions in Teaching Technical Writing," *The Technical Writing Teacher* 9, no. 2 (1982), outlines an effective means of helping students learn in a workshop setting, offering advice on such techniques as group introductions on the first day of class to get students acquainted and talking to one another, effective ways of arranging students in groups, and having students read their papers aloud to one another. Further, Kenneth E. Bruffee's *A Short Course in Writing* (Cambridge, Mass.: Winthrop, 1980) discusses the importance of collaborative learning in the writing process. Bruffee discusses peer criticism as a means of helping students gain audience awareness, and he offers suggestions for a disciplined approach to peer criticism that involves learning to read and respond to a piece of writing in three distinct and different ways: descriptively, evaluatively, and substantively.

Collaborative work has been found effective in teaching composition in general; it is especially effective in the technical writing classroom because it enhances the students' sense of audience and because it teaches students the reality of work in an industrial or business setting where committee and other forms of collaborative work prevail. In the workshop, students learn the social reality of dealing with coworkers.

The Nontechnical Technical Writing Teacher

One of the fears often expressed by new teachers of technical writing, particularly by teachers with a literature background, concerns their lack of technical expertise. Yet this absence of technical background is not necessarily a weakness. Technical writing teachers do not need to be experts in every field. Like the technical editors Don Bush speaks of in "Content Editing, an Opportunity for Growth" (*Technical Communication* 28, no. 4 [1981]), their lack of technical expertise may make them better able to "spot the occasional gaps in engineering logic" (17). Bush concedes that technical editors do need to learn a little jargon in order to be effective as critics. Teachers, too, need to learn a little jargon. But an interested reading of a few technical papers can give teachers a passing familiarity with the language in a discipline. And in the ongoing process of learning, they are apt to ask key questions that make students all the more sensitive to the technical words they are using and their reasons for using them. Thus, teachers can help students learn that although technical jargon has its place if the audience is right, unnecessary jargon should be avoided.

Clearly a teacher with a nontechnical background should never attempt to pose as an authority in a technical field. But the fact that the technical writing teacher is not an authority in a student's field can often lead to a rapport between student and teacher that enhances the learning process for both. The fact that students are the authorities in their fields enhances their self-esteem, so that the teacher's role as the writing authority becomes less threatening. Because they can maintain self-esteem in the face of criticism of their writing, students often learn more readily, and they are then more likely to leave the technical writing course with healthy attitudes toward writing or English courses.

One of the strongest advantages of not being immersed in students' disciplines is that teachers can serve as lay readers. At the lower-division level, most of students' work is not highly technical. They are writing to the nonspecialist. At this point in their education, students who can be taught to write with clarity for a lay audience can come a long way toward an understanding of writing and of their disciplines, an understanding that can lead to greater clarity in writing for specialists.

Research in Technical Writing

The novice technical writing teacher should lay his or her fears aside and look forward to the challenge technical writing offers. As Don Bush says, "Technical writing is a marvelous laboratory for the study of English. Here we see the very latest language from science, from business, from the military, from government, from academia, and from computerland" ("Content Editing," 16). The technical writing teacher should welcome this opportunity to see language in its formative state, to learn how jargon may be useful, to help govern the invention of new words.

The literature major, educated to analyze, to research, and to write, can appreciate the challenge of the work to be done in the field of technical writing. We need to find ways to bring more of the research being done in psycholinguistics, in communication, and in rhetoric into the technical writing classroom. Other areas that need to be explored include the effects of the use of various forms of figurative language on the readability and comprehensibility of scientific and technical writing. One such study reported by Annette Norris Bradford at the Twenty-Ninth International Technical Communication Conference ("A Research Design to Test the Effectiveness of the Rhetorical Schemes in Enhancing the Comprehensibility of Scientific/Technical Writing," *Proceedings, Twenty-Ninth International Technical Communication Conference* [Washington, D.C.: Society for Technical Communication, 1982]) hypothesizes that the use of figures of speech aids in comprehensibility because variation in syntactic arrangement "add[s] regularity of structure and create[s] and fulfill[s] patterns of expectation" (E-21). Described in the same proceedings are Susan Feinberg's research on the correlation of writing apprehension and writing performance in technical writing courses at the Illinois Institute of Technology ("Recent Research on Writer's Apprehension and Writer's Performance") and Maria Curro Kreppel's application of literary techniques to the evaluation of technical writing ("Help from the Literary Critics in Determining Technical Style"). In addition, Philip M. Rubens, in "Needed Research in Technical Communication: A Report from the Front," cites "creation and dissemination of information" as the "most dominant feature" (E-100) of our society and calls for systematic research in (1) the writing process as it applies to professional writing; (2) the impact of technological change (in the form of videodiscs, word processors, and laser control of printing processes) on "the ways in which we perceive both writing and the texts we create" (E-101); and (3) the reading processes of adult readers and the effect of electronic texts on the reader.

Another call for research is contained in "Research in Technical and Scientific Communication," by Paul V. Anderson, R. John Brockmann, and Carolyn R. Miller. This essay introduces their anthology *New Essays in Technical Communication: Research, Theory, Practice* (Farmingdale, N.Y.: Baywood, 1983). Anderson, Brockmann, and Miller suggest possibilities for the contextual study of technical and scientific communication "in terms of the disciplines that employ it, of historical circumstances in which it has arisen and developed, of the offices and laboratories and shops in which it is produced and used" (13). Literature majors should find particularly interesting two essays in this anthology: James Stephens's "Style as Therapy in Renaissance Science," and James Paradis's "Bacon, Linnaeus, and Lavoisier: Early Language Reform in the Sciences." These essays point to the research potential of the literature of science and technology, a corpus of writings that in large part have been ignored by critics of language and literature.

Clearly there is much work to be done in the field of technical writing. And literature majors, with a slight shift in orientation, are well prepared to move into this challenging field. As Carol Yee points out in her response to a panel titled "What Beginning Teachers Should Know about Business and Technical Writing" (in *Technical Communications: Perspectives for the Eighties*), technical writing teachers need not abandon the humanities in order to teach students to write in their professions. Indeed, they can and should bring their training in the humanities—their appreciation for the language, their awareness of cultural heritage, their ability to see the connections between science and technology and the humanities, and most of all their ability to write—into the technical writing classroom. Let us welcome this opportunity to share the humanism of literature and the study of language with students and professionals in technical and scientific fields.

The Great Commandment

John J. Ruszkiewicz
University of Texas at Austin

If I were asked to formulate a single directive for inexperienced teachers of freshman English, a commandment summarizing all the lore and scholarship in the field of composition, it would be this: Above all, teach writing. I believe that no other piece of advice would have been more valuable to me a decade ago, during my first semester as a writing instructor, had I been able to perceive how radical and yet how elegant a solution to the problems I faced this unassuming guideline could be. Then more than now, much of what went on in a typical freshman composition course was only tangentially related to the goal of improving a student's ability to write. I remember opening my first freshman English class at Ohio State by explaining to twenty-four terrified students that Aristotle had divided all oratory into deliberative, forensic, and epideictic types. In subsequent meetings, I dutifully taught syllogisms, enthymemes, topoi, artistic and inartistic proofs—even the merit of evidence obtained through torture—and distributed lengthy lists of barely pronounceable schemes and tropes, including such useful devices as epenthesis, aphaeresis, and apocope. During the semester I also talked about the history of the language, the nature of metaphor, and the production of Johnson's dictionary and the O.E.D. As a class we discussed politics, film criticism, English literature, advertising, and Latin grammar and syntax. Week after week I invented material to fill up the hours allotted to talking about writing, borrowing whenever I could from friends and colleagues no less reluctant to ride an intellectual hobbyhorse, nor better informed about what freshman English should be. During that first semester, I was actually taking two "rhetoric-related" graduate courses, one a history of rhetoric and the other a seminar on teaching composition. The former stocked me with categories, terms, figures, and structures which I neatly repackaged for my students; the latter convinced me of the importance of what I was trying to accomplish in English 100. But neither led me to consider how well I was doing what I was being paid to do. Enthusiastic and well-intentioned, I shared with my colleagues an apocalyptic dream that English 100 was supposed to be a synopsis of Western culture or the point at which students made a commitment to the English language as their personal savior. But somewhere between paeans to language study and lectures on oxymoron and anaphora, the simple imperative to teach writing kept getting lost.

Teaching Writing

I am now convinced that writing can be taught well in different ways. I know many teachers who successfully combine seemingly disparate materials on the history of the language, linguistics, rhetorical theory, politics, and literary study with practical instruction in writing, but such amalgamations are ordinarily achieved only after years of experience and experimentation. Consequently, until instructors have spent a lot of time with students—reading their essays, marking their drafts, listening to their questions, solving their problems—I recommend that they restrict what goes on in a writing classroom to what fits comfortably under a rather basic notion of teaching writing, to russet yeas and honest kersey noes.

Applying this advice is not always easy, particularly for graduate students in English trained to discover and admire subtle and esoteric relationships between ideas and language. I can without much difficulty imagine sincere teachers arguing wittily that a knowledge of the great vowel shift is essential to a student's ability to spell, or idealistically that no student can expect to write clear, modern prose without being exposed to Milton, Swift, Dryden, Woolf, Johnson, Thoreau, Sontag, or a dozen other prose stylists. Yet neither ingenuity nor idealism ought to wield the razor in deciding what is left in or out of a writing course. Instead, instructors need a persistent and tough inner voice to register caution whenever they find themselves pontificating on subjects that most of their students will not find obviously related to the problems they face in writing an essay.

The problem for new instructors as well as for many experienced teachers returning to the writing classroom after sojourns in literature courses is figuring out what to teach. I have heard the question put this way: What am I supposed to talk about for fifty minutes every day if I don't have some "stuff" to analyze—a poem, short story, drama, historical movement, critical genre, school of artists, notorious figure? Lectures on grammar and spelling? Discussions of modes of discourse? Analyses of model essays? At first blush the obvious answer again is frustratingly cryptic: The content of any writing course ought to be writing.

Generally, what you, as a new instructor, should do in setting up a course in composition is, so far as possible, to design a class that sparks the invention of ideas, that encourages exploration of structures and styles, that heightens students' awareness of audience and purpose, that stimulates, even requires, reassessment and revision, and that simulates the procedures professional writers employ in doing their work. The writing produced by students in this kind of course—the essays, journals, research papers, themes, paragraphs—become not mere assignments turned in at regular intervals for a grade, but the heart and soul of the entire term. And students themselves should be treated not as grammatical and stylistic subversives who need to be brought into line for the good of civilization, but as apprentice writers filled with potential.

Stimulating Invention

Students' potential as writers is often least apparent in what they find to say about any given topic—even topics they know a great deal about. In recent years an enormous amount of thought has been given to that aspect of composing which, as early as Aristotle's *Rhetoric,* seemed to be the key to effective communication: invention. Scholars and teachers have created dozens of schemes, lists, matrices, patterns, devices, and questions to stimulate the capacities writers already have for finding topics and developing ideas. It is both disturbing and vaguely comforting that no single system or device seems to have harnessed the creative and imaginative capacities of our students to the extent that it can be counted on to produce thoughtful, fully developed essays every time. Consequently, what you, the teacher, need to know immediately about invention is not how any given system operates but simply that students have to be pushed into a relationship with their subjects that reflects the value that their material—whether it be the raw stuff of an essay on summer employment, Milton's *Lycidas,* or Reaganomics—will have for them and for their potential readers. I am not saying that students should be asked to write only about those things which interest them, because writers often must produce good work about subjects they care little about. Instead, inexperienced writers need to be taught to probe into the recesses of any subject to discover what there is that is surprising, informative, pleasurable, or useful to a reader. For this reason, there can be no lists of "sure-fire, can't-miss" topics, because the subject a student chooses is almost always less important than the treatment he or she will give it. For the novice instructor who has not yet had the opportunity to read *De Inventione* or discover tagmemics, the key to teaching invention is to ask questions, to stimulate controversy, and to encourage exploration. Too simple? Many new teachers panic when class discussions run out of control, past the time allotted to them, because heated debates and spirited dialectics can seem shapeless, directionless, and wasteful. But when discussions are focused on what students are writing about, the noise and heat generated are the best evidence that invention is taking place and the best catalysts for composition I know of.

Of course, you cannot debate every essay topic your students will have, but you can through individual comments and group work comment on many of the topic ideas students float. Both you and your students should be honest in assessing a topic—after all, you are critical audiences. Tell students when they are treading ground that is already worn bare, or treating ideas too simply or naively. Let them know that there is a library full of fact and opinion waiting to amplify what they believe and know. And don't let personal experiences substitute—time and again—for research, thought, and creativity.

Developing Structure and Style

Teaching writing also means helping students compose coherent, well-organized pieces in appropriate styles, but the most effective way of getting them to write well is not to describe good prose to them but to give them samples of writing to read and evaluate—particularly their own. Many experienced teachers of writing will admit that there is, after all, not much you can say about organizing essays that has an immediate and salutary effect on what students do. Long lists of clever openings and closings, elaborate essay paradigms, meticulous outlines, and testimonies to the structural integrity of the classical oration have only remote connections to the way students—or teachers—tend to organize what they write. Most instructors tend to vacillate in the way they teach arrangement between periods of organicism, during which they expect students to discover on their own appropriate forms for their essays, and reactive periods of formalism, during which they require students to produce vigorously crafted pieces with topic sentences exactly here, points of development exactly there, dutiful conclusions, and tough little transitional words at every conceivable juncture. These swings between structural anarchy and structural "fascism" really reflect a truism: that most writers rely on a bit of constraint and a bit of caprice to get themselves and their readers from one end of a page to the other. Teaching writing means that instead of describing structural paradigms, or breaking Antony's lament for Caesar into all its components, or ferreting out topic sentences in endless fields of paragraphs, you should spend time in class reading your students' essays and having them read one another's work, pointing out where the ideas move nicely along, and where readers might get lost. Discuss and revise openings that are too abrupt, conclusions that do not work, and middles of essays that need more development or are just plain confusing. Instead of simply listing transitions, show students how to use them. The same direct approach works with teaching style. Put a variety of student paragraphs on the board and work on them, adding grace and pruning wordiness. Don't lecture. I wish I could have back all the classes I wasted describing high, middle, and low styles and the proper occasions for their use.

Of course, structure and style in writing depend upon audience and purpose. These days it is hard to find a composition teacher who does not swear by audience and purpose. But until you have had the time to become familiar with the ample literature that treats these aspects of composing, you can be comfortable in knowing that the classroom implications of all the research and scholarship boil down to rather simple advice for your students: to write well, they must reckon with audience and purpose. You will find that while you can lecture on audience and purpose effectively for about ten minutes, you will be teaching these concepts in students' drafts and essays for your entire career.

Designing an Effective Writing Course

Teaching writing requires you to concentrate on what your students are writing, to make their thoughts, their topics, their drafts, their experiments, their revisions the focal points of your course. What you need to do is *show* them how to be better writers, to work along with them. You need to set up your course to allow them to think, write, comment, evaluate, and revise right there in your classroom so they will be prepared to do the same in their dorm rooms, offices, and homes. Their written products are the investment they have in your course and the proper subject matter of it. A lecture about Seneca's influence on Renaissance prose or Newman's concept of a university education may at first glance seem more substantive than fifty minutes of silent composing, but that is probably a judgment shaped by a reading of audience and purpose based on courses other than freshman English. Until you overcome these feelings of guilt about not teaching specific content in a composition class, you are likely to struggle as a teacher of writing, and many of your students will be confused and frustrated.

There are dozens of ways to set up effective courses that encourage the teacher and students both to explore the process of writing. The course designs I prefer are those which allow teachers to intervene and comment on essays while they are still in the draft stage and which delay the assigning of a grade until a student decides that a given piece is finished. Most writing-centered courses also encourage some collaboration between students on projects, frequent peer-group editing, and a great deal of feedback and self-assessment. In any type of course, encourage revision. Perhaps the only stupid question an *experienced* teacher of writing can ask is "Should I allow my students to revise?" You are not teaching writing if you are not allowing revision.

The simple imperative to teach writing suggests the relative importance of much else that typically occurs in a composition course. Grammar exercises for their own sake are wasted energy; when they address immediate and repeated student needs, they become essential. Specific skills and routines that contribute to effective writing of a given kind (proper paper format, accurate footnote form) are appropriate measures for evaluation; those that are not (tardiness, listlessness, bent corners in lieu of staples) can be ignored. Assignments that have a point and a specific audience in mind are likely to be more productive than those that stem from theoretical systems or a teacher's personal preferences. If you continue on as a composition instructor, you will have plenty of time to explore ways of teaching writing that incorporate intellectual perspectives and subject matters not mentioned or championed here. For first-time teachers I would offer this advice: Keep your enthusiasm high, your expectations reasonable, and your focus on what you are asking your students to do. In short, teach writing.

Writing Right Off:
Strategies for Invention

Mary Jane Schenck
University of Tampa

As teachers of writing, we all want to foster the type of spontaneity and imagination that leads to lively papers. We are therefore slightly chagrined when we hear, in response to what we believe is a creative assignment, "I don't have any ideas." Being the articulate and even glib people we English teachers usually are, we are quick to offer many helpful suggestions. But each time we supply the topic, point the direction, or pose all the questions, we cut off the possibility that students will reach into themselves and discover the sources of their own thinking and feeling. The desire—some might even say the compulsion—to organize a class to the second and maintain a position of complete authority is unfortunately common to veteran as well as novice teachers, but it is at least understandable in the inexperienced ones. The first few classes can be an intimidating situation for a young or inexperienced teacher. A normal response is to overprepare, to take charge, and to feel totally responsible for everything that occurs.

Being one of those who has tended to overprepare over the years, I would not advocate a nonchalance about class preparation that results in wasted class time and cynical students. What I suggest, however, in place of the teacher-centered, tightly organized class, is a series of carefully thought-out situations that allow students to work out their own processes of invention—not the instructor's. I think we too often take all the initiative and set the parameters of a discussion without realizing that our questions and topics can become *perimeters* and actually circumscribe the debate. Students may lose track of ideas or reactions they might have had that are important to address and perhaps of more interest to them than our own sophisticated perspectives.

In our composition courses at the University of Tampa, we assign readings or have students see films to generate discussion and provide interesting topics for them to use as writing assignments. Although we require only a brief reading list, discourage lecturing, and encourage all instructors to focus primarily on the process of writing, these courses

84

are similar to content courses in literature or sociology in that they have a body of material to react to. I would defend the inclusion of a definite content in a composition course, for it provides much-needed intellectual stimulation and makes these courses potentially as interesting and challenging as any other academic course. But the temptation for all of us, veterans and novices alike, is to fill class time with the sound of our own voices. We are a bit afraid of silence in response to our questions, so we rush to supply answers or rambling restatements of the same questions—and we are even more afraid of student-centered activities that leave us out entirely.

Yet, if we are to take seriously the importance of invention in the writing process, we will be well advised to set up situations that encourage students to take the responsibility for their own processes of invention and discovery. A good reading or a thought-provoking film is an excellent preparation for class, but the opening of the class session itself should emphasize writing as a mode of responding to and analyzing what has been read or seen. The prewriting strategies that follow are especially appropriate to use as openers for any class or at any point when the class is ready to take up new material.

Journals

Having students keep journals is excellent writing practice and will provide a constant source of ideas and student writing for instructors and students to use in classes. Instructors may want to specify the number of entries per week, the amount of time to be spent making entries, and the general focus of the entries. It is also important to let students know that these are public journals, if the instructor intends to use them in class. The students can devise a system (e.g., pages folded over) to shield from public view any entries that stray into completely personal territory. They also need to know that a journal is not a diary or a list of everything they did during the day. Entries can be reactions to the readings and films for the course, to hot topics in the news and on campus, or to material being studied in other classes. Students can use entries to generate ideas, solve problems, or merely reflect on what is going on around them. The important thing to stress is that the journal is a place to record reactions, ideas, and feelings of significance to the student.

I would have students keep journals in notebooks separate from class notes and have the journals brought to class every day. Several students can be asked to read their entries on a given reading assignment aloud to start off a class discussion. These entries give the instructor marvelous insight into what the students have made of their reading and what they find important or puzzling. The conflicting reactions to and interpretations of the material will also give the students a genuine example of the phenomenology of reading, or "reader response." Even if the discussion which follows is instructor-led, the questions posed or the issues raised can be set by the students themselves at the outset, leading all of them to greater involvement (we can always make our own bright points later). Journal entries can also be exchanged and used as samples of student writing for any number of exercises—rewriting for different audiences, hunting for main ideas and supporting detail, or identifying expressive language. Most important, students can use their own journal entries as starting points for longer pieces of writing. They can pick out the most interesting entry for the week and expand it, or a peer reader can be asked to suggest the most interesting entries.

Free-writing

Two varieties of this exercise—undirected free-writing and guided free-writing—offer instructors another excellent way to open class. Students may be resistant at first to directions like "Write whatever comes into your minds and don't stop writing," but they will soon enter into the spirit if they are told to keep the pen moving, even if it means writing the same word over and over again or writing "This is dumb" until new thoughts enter their minds. It is important to limit the time spent on such an exercise (five to ten minutes) and for the instructor to write at the same time. If several of the students are asked to read their free-writing aloud, the instructor should share his or hers as well, especially when first using this exercise in a class. Donald Murray suggests that instructors be willing to do public writing on the blackboard while students write. It is very useful for them to see the hesitations, repetitions, awkward phrasing, or whatever else emerges from the pen or chalk of an "authority." The instructor should go over the piece with the students, commenting on what was surprising, what seemed to go well, and what seems to be unrelated and best abandoned, allowing students to see critical reading as well as writing. In this way students will see not only how imperfect an instructor's writing can be but will also see at work the critical reading skills they need to acquire.

Guided free-writing is an excellent way to begin a discussion—a provocative question about the reading or a key word will draw everyone into the material at hand and away from the preceding class or personal preoccupations. If the instructor merely starts a discussion, one or two students will respond and the others will think they have nothing to say or will be convinced, having heard the others, that what they were going to say was stupid. Given five or ten minutes to pull their thoughts together and put them in writing, they are more likely to feel secure about reading them aloud or referring to them later during the discussion. One of the major benefits of free-writing is, of course, that gems do show up and students can use them later as sources for longer pieces of writing.

Heuristics

The invention phase of writing may just be the most fun, instead of the most frustrating, if the instructor feels comfortable in setting up the tasks and can explain, with concrete examples, just how heuristics can help to generate ideas. Students can be asked to do tree-diagrams, answer the journalist's "who, what, when, where, why" about a topic, or apply Burke's pentad to describe the action, actors, scene, means, and purpose in a topic. Among some of the most familiar and easiest invention strategies are brainstorming or list making; Young, Becker, and Pike's concept of seeing a subject as a particle, wave, or field; force-field analysis; graphics; and a question/answer exercise we call circle writing.[1]

In our composition classes, for instance, we have used Friedrich Dürrenmatt's *The Visit* (filmed by Twentieth-Century Fox in 1964) and Ursula Le Guin's *The Word for World Is Forest*. The following exercises, designed by instructors in the program, illustrate the use of some of these heuristics.[2] Naturally, instructors will find some heuristics more appropriate than others for given material, and one or two would suffice for a class. It is helpful, however, for students to be exposed to as many different strategies during the course as possible, for, as Elaine Maimon has said, "One student's heuristic is another's writing block."[3]

Brainstorming/List Making

Students are asked to spend five minutes writing words or phrases as fast as they can in response to key words or questions. In a second stage of the exercise, they are asked to circle related words or several major ideas that emerge from their lists.

The Visit
  Justice
  Peer pressure in Guellen
  Character traits of Claire

Impact of credit on Guellen

The Word for World Is Forest

Xenophobia

Reactions of settlers in a new land

Qualities of Athshean women

Character traits of one of the major characters

Particle, Wave, and Field

Students are asked to consider individuals or events from three per-spectives—as an isolated, individual person or event (particle), as some-one or something in process (wave), or as a part of a larger network of relationships and circumstances (field).

The Visit

Particle: Analyze Ill's character.

Wave: Look at the changes in Ill and his attitude toward death.

Field: Analyze Ill as a father, husband, citizen, friend, and seducer.

The Word for World Is Forest

Particle: Analyze Davidson or Lyubov as representative of human nature and Selver as a representative Athshean.

Wave: How does each of the major characters change?

Field: Analyze the relationship between the major characters. Are they opposites or complementary, cooperative or competitive?

Word Associations/Analogies

Students are asked to generate lists of words or events called to mind by terms used in a reading or film.

The Visit

Brainstorm examples of present-day communal acts; then search for analogies with the situation in the play or movie (religious rit-uals, fraternity/sorority initiations, committees, corporations).

What do the names of Claire's husbands and companions bring to mind?

The Word for World Is Forest

Look for analogies with the war in Vietnam, British colonialism in Africa or India, American wars against the Indians.

Look at naming in the novel, e.g., Creechies/Athsheans, Scarface/ Selver.

Look for historical or current parallels.

Force-field Analysis

Students can do this graphic analysis of conflicting values in a text individually or in small groups.

The Visit

List as a chart the factors for and against taking Ill's life, from the town's point of view.

Follow-up question: How should the society decide which factors are most important in making this decision?

The Word for World Is Forest

List the positive and negative characteristics of the Yumens and the Athsheans.

Follow-up questions: Which society has more positive qualities? How has the author manipulated the reader into seeing these qualities?

Graphics

Drawing or sketching is an especially good heuristic for students who learn best through a visual mode. But even the less gifted artistically can learn from sketching or laying out diagrams of situations.

The Visit

Sketch the opening scene as you imagine it from the play.

Sketch the town square with Claire on the balcony as depicted in the movie. Can you imagine another setup for those scenes?

Sketch Claire being driven from the town—what are the expressions on people's faces?

The Word for World Is Forest

Sketch caricatures of all the major characters in the novel.

Sketch the Athshean landscape both before and after the arrival of the Yumens.

Circle Writing

Students sit in a circle in small groups or as an entire class, and each student writes a question he or she has thought of while reading the assignment.[4] Students should be cautioned not to ask questions that will require only a yes/no or factual answer. The sheet of paper with the question at the top is passed along to the next student, who is asked to write for five or ten minutes in answer to the question. If desired, a second stage of the process can be used: the paper can be passed to yet another student, who will write a reaction to both the question and the first answer. Only the original question-writer's name need be placed on the sheet, so that it can be returned to him or her. The question-writer should then be asked to write a longer piece based on the original question, using the responses to it to refine, elaborate upon, or change the original question and his or her original thoughts about potential answers to the question. If another feedback loop is desired, then all names should be put on the exercise, so that the original question-writer can show respondents what he or she ultimately did with the question, their reactions to it, and what his or her own opinions are. This exercise is excellent for both prewriting and drafting.

Small-Group Learning

Small-group learning accomplishes several goals in any class. It fosters cooperation and tolerance of others' opinions. It increases the students' ability to formulate and articulate ideas, calling on their own resources for creative or analytical thought rather than merely on their capacity for data acquisition and restatement.[5] In the writing class, small-group learning is especially valuable in prewriting because questions or approaches to issues raised in small-group exercises can immediately be used for first drafts of papers. The groundwork is also laid for the collaborative work on writing involved in peer review, if it is to be used in the class.

The instructor may wish to divide the class or let the students choose their own groups (seven students per group is ideal). If a given group tends not to be productive because of a poor mix of personalities or the presence of too many close friends, the instructor can use an artificial means of regrouping the entire class for subsequent exercises. Students can be grouped by home states, home towns, birthdays—any gimmick the instructor feels will result in a random mix. It is important to let students know that the purpose of small-group work is collaboration and consensus building rather than competitiveness and determining right or wrong answers. They should be informed that they are not expected to use small-group work to learn facts but to analyze, synthesize, or interpret material found in their readings. They must also be able to see by the quality of the process that the small-group exercises are not

time fillers used by the instructor because she or he did not have anything else to do with the class. The instructor should carefully set up
each exercise, announce time limits, leave time at the end for synthesis
of group ideas, point out how the students' ideas are related to the material in question, and point out how they can use their ideas for a writing assignment. It would also help to talk to students or give them a
handout about constructive and destructive roles that individuals play
within a group. Finally, the instructor should make clear how group
work will be evaluated. I have found that, given a little practice with
short exercises, a class will readily take to small-group exercises as a
normal part of each class period. The value becomes apparent to them
as they gain respect for their peers' opinions and feel a growing sense
of the importance of their own, so specific evaluation of each small-
group exercise is not necessary. But it is useful to design several extended small-group projects that will be evaluated for credit to encourage students to work outside of class with their peers and take the
responsibility for a sustained task without the constant intervention of
an instructor.

What follows is a description of several brief group exercises that were
used to generate discussion of works read in our composition classes.
The time limits are only suggestions; instructors should experiment
with different limits to determine which types of group work need more
or less time.

Exercise Based on Readings from B. F. Skinner

1. Individual Brainstorming:
   Think of five things you value very highly. How did they come to
   be of value to you? Who or what influenced the development of
   those values? (5 minutes)

2. Small-group Work, Consensus Building, Nonevaluative Listening,
   Ranking:
   Divide into small groups. Listen to each student's list of five values
   without criticizing. Try to come to a consensus about the origins of
   everyone's values. Then rank the origins or influences from most
   significant to least significant. (10–15 minutes)

3. Large-group Work, Reporting, Consensus Building:
   The recorder from each group will read out results of step 2. The
   whole class then attempts a ranking of origins or influences. (5–10
   minutes)

4. Instructor's Summary:
   Reflect on the students' thinking processes and ask them to com-

pare their ideas with Skinner's statement that values are created
and reinforced by the culture or the environment. (5–10 minutes)

5. Write-up:
   Have students write about their reactions to the discussion—what
   clarification it has brought to their own thinking about values, new
   ideas that occurred to them, and what they would like to write
   about if asked to write a paper on Skinner. (5 minutes)

Exercises Based on Camus's "The Plague"

Exercise A

1. Individual Brainstorming:
   If you were suddenly quarantined and confined to this campus for
   an indeterminate time because of an outbreak of a contagious and
   deadly disease, what do you think you would do? (5 minutes)

2. Small-group Work, Consensus Building, Nonevaluative Listening:
   Divide into groups, and listen to each person's reaction to the question. Try to reach a consensus about the best course of action suggested by the group. (10 minutes)

3. Fishbowl, Consensus Building:
   Choose one representative from each small group and put them
   in the center of the room with their fellow group members seated
   behind them. Have the representatives attempt to reach an agreement on the most valid response to the situation by arguing their
   groups' positions. Time-outs may be called for the representatives
   to get advice from group members. (15 minutes)

4. Instructor's Summary:
   Restate each group's major points and analyze underlying values.
   Point out why consensus was difficult or easy to reach based on the
   range of values represented. Ask for reactions to the fishbowl exercise. What helped or impeded a consensus? (10 minutes)

5. Write-up:
   Have students write about their choices and have them speculate
   about how the discussion altered or confirmed their original positions. (5–10 minutes)

Exercise B

1. Individual Ranking:
   Faced by a situation such as that depicted in *The Plague*, what responses would be best? Rank your responses from 1 to 10. (5
   minutes)

_____ philosophical contemplation

_____ buying things and enjoying them

_____ pursuing an intimate personal relationship with someone

_____ practicing your religion

_____ taking care of others

_____ recording the events for the future

_____ attempting escape

_____ researching the cause of the disease

_____ organizing people to maintain civil order

_____ trying to achieve excellence in something that was always important to you

2. Small-group Work:
   Have the students discuss their reasons for the ordering they have chosen. Have them try to see not only the values underlying their choices but also the connections with the characters in *The Plague* and Camus's point of view on the validity of each response. (Obviously, not all responses will parallel the text.)

3. Small-group Work, Nonevaluative Listening, Ranking:
   Divide into small groups and listen to each member's ranking. Discuss what values seem to be behind the choices made. Come to a consensus about a group ranking of responses from most valuable to least valuable, on a scale of 1 to 10. (15 minutes)

4. Large-group Work:
   Have a recorder from each group read aloud the results of the group ranking. Discuss the values behind the choices and what made consensus easy or difficult. (10 minutes)

5. Instructor's Summary:
   Point out any values that seem to be unclear to the students. Have them identify which characters in the novel have the responses in the original list (remembering that not all are exactly parallel). (10 minutes)

6. Write-up:
   As in exercise A. (5–10 minutes)

Whatever mixture of prewriting or small-group learning exercises is selected, the composition class is invariably enriched by such student-centered activities. By using these exercises as openers, we convey the important message to the students that their ideas and feelings are at the center of the class. Good writing must spring from personal experience and personal conviction, in the sense that both concrete experience and abstract concepts must become the students' own before they can write well about them. Most of the invention strategies mentioned here are aimed precisely at making ideas that may originate in another's work ultimately the students' own as they struggle to understand, react to, and formulate new ideas through interaction with peers. Naturally, these strategies are not the only ones to create student involvement; we need only think of common assignments such as letter writing, peer interviewing, and writing for self-discovery that could also be used to ensure that students write from a sense of conviction and personal knowledge about their subjects.[6] The role of the teacher at this point is to allow the students' own processes of invention to work. By remaining in the background in the early stages, the teacher helps students to develop more self-confidence about starting all writing assignments, especially outside of class. The students will also be primed, by these opening exercises, to attend to what should be the primary focus of the class—reading and responding to drafts of student work that have grown out of previous sessions on invention. At that point, when it is appropriate, the teacher will play a more active role by demonstrating good critical reading and editing skills.

Notes

1. An excellent source for explanations and illustrations of these and other heuristics is *Writing in the Arts and Sciences,* by Elaine Maimon, Gerald Belcher, Gail Hearn, Barbara Nodine, and Finbarr O'Connor (Boston: Little, Brown, 1981). For Young, Becker, and Pike's concept of particle, wave, and field, see Richard E. Young, Alton L. Becker, and Kenneth L. Pike, *Rhetoric: Discovery and Change* (New York: Harcourt Brace Jovanovich, 1970). Other useful sources for teachers are Donald Murray, *Learning for Teaching* (Montclair, N.J.: Boynton/ Cook, 1982); Erika Lindemann, *A Rhetoric for Teachers* (New York: Oxford Univ. Press, 1983).

2. The exercises on *The Visit* and *The Word for World Is Forest* were designed by Professors Frank Gillen, Suzanne Nelson, and Mary Jane Schenck.

3. *Writing in the Arts and Sciences,* instructor's manual, 21.

4. I first heard of this exercise from Professors Julie Empric and Richard Mathews.

5. There are many published sources on small-group learning. I am especially indebted for my ideas to Professors Edward Glassman and Eugene Watson, who have directed several workshops for our faculty. See also Edward Glassman, "The Teacher as Leader," *New Directions for Teaching and Learning* 1 (1980): 61–70.

6. Thanks to Professor Jo Ann Valenti for responding to a draft of this paper and for reminding me of these useful assignments.

Planning for Spontaneity in the Writing Classroom and a Passel of Other Paradoxes

Ronald F. Lunsford
Clemson University

Last semester one of my students produced a rough draft of an essay which began with the following paragraph:

> I am now a first year college student and throughout all of my school years I have witnessed, like any teenager, every kind, shape, and form of teacher possible. Some were terrible, most were mediocre, and then there are always the outstanding few, one of whom this paper is devoted. She was my twelfth grade English teacher. Her name was Mrs. Knapp and the course she taught was "Great Books." The way she taught was like no way that I had ever been subjected too. It was fantastic. I learned more in that one year course than any other class that I had taken.

After this draft was read and reviewed by one of his classmates, the student produced a final draft of the essay, which began as follows:

> "Hey all you schnerts out there, listen up!" she blared, "we need to get class started, so form a circle." This was a typical beginning of one of my favorite classes of all times. The course was "Great Books," taught by the fantastic Mrs. Knapp. Her method of teaching was like nothing I had ever been subjected to, yet it was wonderful. I am now a firm believer in her style of teaching because I learned more in that one course than in any other course I have ever taken.

The paper which followed this introduction was flawed; it was far from perfect. But it stands out in my mind as one of the best revisions I have seen in a writing class, and I am convinced that the paper's success can be traced to the role that peer-group critiques play in my writing course. These critiques do not work magically; the teacher must plan carefully before using them if they are to work.

I recently began a workshop for writing teachers by asking them to list all the problems they might encounter should they decide to use group critiques in their writing classes:

Students can plagiarize from each other.

Students can be too hard on one another's writing.

Students can be too easy on one another's writing.

Students can take bad advice from peers.

Students can fail to heed helpful advice from peers.

Students can dominate group sessions.

Students can refuse to contribute in the sessions.

Given all of the ways in which group critiques can fail, it is not hard to see why many teachers either have never tried them or have given up on them after an initial unsuccessful attempt to use them. This is especially true for teachers new to the classroom. But there are those of us who continue to use groups year after year despite these potential problems. Why? And what techniques have we developed to reduce the risks involved?

We use groups to help students begin to view writing as a process because group work emphasizes revision. Whether the members of groups see a paper only once before it is turned in to the instructor or see it at two or more stages of development, the critiquing process suggests that writers must revise their pieces. Even if peers do not see the writing a second time, the teacher will see the draft that was submitted to peers and will compare it to the final draft. Thus, he or she can determine whether the final draft represents revision or recopying.

All too often, students confuse these two activities. Students may be required to submit a rough draft, but if no one responds to that draft, they can easily fall into the trap of editing—correcting only grammatical and mechanical errors—when they should be revising—rewriting to make meaning become clear. The peer-group critique ensures that writers will get responses to their drafts, and these responses make it harder for them to see their task in producing a final draft as nothing more than "copying over in ink."

In addition to enabling us to focus on the writing process, peer groups allow us to engage students in their own learning. Students teach themselves as they teach their peers. I am convinced that there is a close relationship between being able to analyze the strengths and weaknesses of a piece of writing and being able to produce good writing. This is not to say that one's ability to write will always match her ability to analyze, but if a student continues to sharpen her analytical skills, her writing will improve as well.

Peer groups also allow weaker students to see the writing of their more able classmates. It is one thing for a teacher to tell a weaker student that his writing is basically correct but lacking in development or voice. It is another for that student to see writing from his peers with that development and voice.

These are at least some of the benefits of groups—unless something goes wrong. But the list of their potential problems above may well cause us to question their real value. They sound good in theory, but if the groups do not work in practice, we are right back where we started. The crucial question, then, is "How do we make them work?" As the title of this essay suggests, group critiques require much planning on the part of the teacher.

I suspect that many teachers miss this important principle because group work looks so effortless on the surface. When one first sees a successful peer-group session, the process does look like magic. In one group, a student is telling another that a particular paragraph seems out of place. In another group, a student is asking a writer just how she wants to make her audience feel and then beginning to describe how he felt as he read the piece in question. In yet another group, a student is commenting that the connotation of a particular word does not seem appropriate and suggesting another word which the writer immediately recognizes as better. And the teacher observes, moving from group to group, serving as a consultant only when she is called upon.

In such a situation, an observer is likely to overlook the teacher's role in this process and may well attribute the success to the excellence of the students rather than to any method employed by the teacher. Paradoxically, while all of this looks very spontaneous (and in one sense of the word, it is), the spontaneity is the result of the teacher's careful planning. Successful critique sessions do not just happen.

The All-Important Plan

Below I will outline the method I use to prepare my students for group work. I would not expect anyone to follow my procedures slavishly; I have certainly adapted the critique plans of other teachers to suit my own style of teaching. Many different plans will work; the key is that there be a plan—that teachers spend time in preparing students for the task at hand.

Let me begin by giving an overview of my plan before discussing what I see as its most important elements. In a typical freshman course, I expect to receive seven or eight papers. One of these is usually a diagnostic paper, one is a final examination, and two or three are in-class writing assignments; thus, I have time for only three extended out-of-class writing assignments. In these assignments, students are required to follow a writing process which includes prewriting, a planning page, an audience analysis, a rough draft, and a final draft. Writing groups are used extensively throughout this process. Students meet in groups to discuss their topics while they are in the midst of prewriting for their papers; they also meet to discuss planning pages and audience analyses. When we reach the rough draft stage, however, the procedure changes somewhat.

The change at this stage is a recent development in my method. Before, I had assumed that as we worked our way through each assignment, every student had to present a draft of his paper to his writing group and receive feedback on it before producing a final draft. In order to complete these critiques, groups were limited to ten minutes per paper. This was simply not enough time for students to respond to one another's papers, but the only alternative that I could see involved spending what seemed an inordinate amount of time in the critiquing process.

I was struggling with this problem when I heard another writing teacher suggest that students did not have to receive group feedback on all of their papers. I immediately saw a solution to my problem. Since I require three long assignments, I divided each of my writing groups into thirds. A third of the group (usually two students) submits a draft of the paper in question to the group for review; a third submits a draft to me; and a third is given no formal review of that draft. This is not to suggest that members of this group cannot seek assistance if they want to, but the assumption is that they will benefit from the process of reviewing the papers of their peers. After all, if they cannot begin to apply the principles enunciated in groups to their own papers, the entire group process is questionable. The effect of this plan, then, is to provide students with a formal review at the draft stage of two of the three out-of-class assignments in the course.

Students are familiar with the procedures of this method and they know well in advance what kinds of help they will receive in writing each paper. When a student is to receive a group critique of her paper, she brings a copy of her draft for each member of the group to the class meeting prior to the critique session. Group members then write responses to the papers to be critiqued before coming to the critique session. (See Appendix for a sample critique sheet.) During the critique session, each paper is discussed for approximately thirty minutes. The writer begins by reading her paper aloud to the group. Then other group members offer suggestions for revision based on the work they have done in reviewing the paper the night before. When the session is completed, reviewers give their written comments to the writer, and the writer then produces her final draft and submits to me all materials generated in the writing process, including the reviews she has received from group members.

This, then, is the procedure in rough form. As I mentioned above, certain key features warrant further discussion. Perhaps I should begin by commenting on the size of groups. An average-sized composition class of twenty-three to twenty-five students will consist of four groups of approximately six members each. These groups are larger than the ones I used when I assumed that all students had to receive critiques for each assignment. But the smaller groups were often totally dysfunctional. In a group of only three members, two of the three must be able to work effectively in group sessions if the method is to succeed, but in a group of six, two or even three weaker students do not necessarily prevent the group from functioning.

Once the groups are formed, students must be trained to critique papers. The training takes two forms in my class: one short-term and the other long. Early on in the semester, I introduce students to peer critiques by having a selected group perform for the class in what we call a "fishbowl" experience. (I took both the term and the idea from Beverly Varnado, a teacher at Wando High School in Mt. Pleasant, South Carolina.) Before this session, I talk about the group-critique process with the students who are going to perform. We decide what paper will be reviewed. If one of them is working on an essay which he would like to use in the session, we critique that paper; if not, I will provide a paper from a previous class and ask one of the students to play the role of writer. In the "fishbowl" experience, the students demonstrate the group-critique process for the rest of the class. The writer (or person playing the role of writer) reads the paper in question. Afterward, members of the group begin by pointing to the particular strengths of the paper. Then they offer suggestions as to how the paper might be made better. They point to passages that are unclear and/or to sentences that might be improved. They may even focus on individual word choices which could be better. After the group has completed its review of the paper, we discuss the critique process as a class, dealing with some of the problems that may arise.

The long-term training involves critique sheets I devise for each essay (see Appendix). In the class before a group critique, I introduce students to a critique sheet designed for that assignment by asking them to critique a draft which has been turned in to me. Remember that approximately a third of the students in the class will submit a draft of each out-of-class essay to me for review. Since these drafts are due at the class meeting before I introduce the critique sheet, I am able to read them and choose one which should prove particularly instructive to the class as a whole. At the beginning of this class meeting, I give all students a copy of the essay and the critique sheet we will use for this assignment. They spend half the period analyzing this sample essay as practice for the critiques they will do of papers by members of their writing groups. We then spend the second half of the class discussing this sample essay, paying particular attention to the kinds of comments that should prove most helpful to the writer in her revising process.

In directing this discussion, I attempt a difficult balancing act. I obviously know more about what makes for successful writing than the students do, but it is important for the students themselves to respond to the drafts we are examining. Therefore, I am as open as possible to the comments individual students make in response to this draft. If a student offers what I see as bad advice, I wait for other students to counter it. In the event that good advice is not forthcoming, however, I do offer my opinion and explain my reasons for holding it as best I can.

One final element in the critiquing process merits some explanation. I mentioned above that students begin critique sessions by reading their papers aloud. For a good many years, I used group critiques without insisting upon this practice. It might seem a small thing, but when I began to stipulate that papers be read aloud, the quality of critique sessions seemed to improve dramatically. I am convinced the improvement was at least in part due to this change, for two reasons. In the first place, no matter how well the writer's peers have done their homework, they need to review an essay before beginning to critique it. As the paper is read, students remember their reactions to it. In the second place, writers can develop a stronger sense of responsibility by reading aloud. Their papers cannot be dashed off, turned in to a teacher, and forgotten; students have to listen to their own papers as they read them. It is common for a student to stop in midsentence to exclaim: "This sentence is terrible!"

Results

At the beginning of this essay, I offered a brief example of what can be accomplished in group critiques. Below I would like to offer a second example. The final draft is not particularly impressive, but the process by which the writer produced that draft is. My point in presenting such an essay is to show the kinds of improvement even an average writer can make following peer review.

The essay was written as a final examination for a freshman writing course. The writer was responding to a prompt that asked her to choose the best teacher she had ever had and to "show" why that teacher was excellent. She wrote a draft of her essay before coming to the final. During the first hour of the exam, she exchanged drafts with a class member, and they critiqued each other's work. Then, she produced her final draft in the remaining two hours of the examination period.

Draft (untitled)

The major purpose of teaching is to have the students learn. There are few teachers who have what it takes to be an effective teacher and can accomplish the goal of having students learn.

The teacher must, first of all, convince the students that he knows the material he is teaching, and earn their respect.

The bell rang for my 9:30 Physics class to begin. As Mr. Wilson walked in, a blanket of silence covered the room. The only noise to be heard was that of his heavy footsteps moving toward his desk. He spoke to that class and then began to lecture. This went on for about one week. It was his way of letting us know that he knew what he was doing and earning our respect.

Then he expressed what his objectives for the class were. They were to understand the basic principles (concepts) of physics, to develop an understanding of problem solving, to do our best and keep up. We accepted his goals and tried to work toward achieving them. He always made sure that he was getting his message across to us. One day class started as usual and Mr. Wilson decided to check everyone's homework. This was fine, but not very many people had theirs.

This got him slightly upset. He wrote these grades in his book. About a week later, he checked homework again and everyone had it so the people who didn't have it the first time received credit and those who did received extra credit. This was his way of knowing that he had gotten his message across.

Also when lecturing, Mr. Wilson would use examples that were funny and related to our lives to communicate effectively with us.

Another one of his concerns was that all of his students had a reasonable understanding of the material. If he felt that your grades were not as high as they should be, he'd ask you to stay after school, otherwise, it was optional whether you stayed or not. Also, everyday, he'd review the previous days work and answer any questions we had.

To make Physics fun was a difficult task, I'm sure, but some days Mr. Wilson would have experiments set up for us to observe, participate in, and enjoy. Also, somedays he would tell us about his adventures hiking in the mountains and caring for his honey bees.

Mr. Wilson was respected by his students and made them really want to learn. Although many students were intimidated by him, Mr. Wilson was an effective teacher to me. He kept me on my toes, provided me with the extra help I sometimes needed, and made physics interesting and fun to learn.

The author received the following response to her draft:

Dear [writer's first name]:

It seems that you have a good start on this paper, but you need to develop your ideas more. There are places that this paper has potential if the ideas were more detailed. I really like paragraph 3. The detail about the blanket of silence and the sounds of the heavy footsteps is great. It makes me feel as if I'm there.

I feel that the thesis is clear because you tell about Mr. Wilson throughout the paper, but again you need to give more detail. For your introduction, you need to catch the reader's attention more. As the introduction is now, the reader has a difficult time getting involved in the paper. Maybe if you gave a personal experience first, the reader could get more involved. I feel the same way about the conclusion. You need something that stands out, and something that the reader will remember.

Your paragraphing does not seem effective, and you also need better transition between paragraphs. It seems that paragraphs 3 and 4 could be combined because I don't see why you started a new paragraph at the point you started it. Why did you start a new paragraph after paragraph 4? At the end of paragraph 4 you tell about the homework incident, and at the beginning of paragraph 5 you are still talking about the homework incident. You don't need to begin a new paragraph there. These are places where I have trouble with your paragraphing. Either you need to combine some of these paragraphs or make them more detailed. If you keep them separate, you need to use transition.

There are also several places where I have questions about what you have written. In paragraph 2, your sentence, "the teacher must convince . . . their respect" is misleading. Aren't there other ways that the teacher can gain respect other than knowing the material? In paragraph 3, your sentence "This went on for about a week" is misleading. Did he teach for a week without stopping? In paragraph 4, what do you mean by this was fine, or who was it fine for? In paragraph 5, the 3rd sentence, I seem to get lost in the long sentence. You need to make it into 2 sentences. Also in paragraph 3, how did the students know that he knew what he was doing? In paragraph 1, it seems that you could say "what it takes" in a different way. Maybe you could say, few teachers have these qualities.

[name of writer], you need to give more detail and develop your ideas more. Paragraph more effectively and use better transition.

Sincerely,

[name of reviewer]

P.S. You picked a good audience.

When the writer received her review, she produced the following final draft:

An Effective Teacher

The main purpose of teaching is to have students learn. There are few teachers who have all of the qualities necessary to be an effective teacher and achieve the goal of having students learn. A good, effective teacher is one to whom students can relate, trust in, and respect. Mr. Wilson is an ideal example of an effective teacher.

The bell rang for my 9:30 Physics class to begin. As Mr. Wilson entered, a blanket of silence covered the room. The only noise to be heard was that of his heavy footsteps moving towards his desk. This being the first day, he explained what the course was going to be about and what was expected to be accomplished in the course. With a smile on his face, he asked, "Can we do it people?" We responded positively and had free time the rest of the period to glance over the book.

Mr. Wilson taught only "high" students and served as an example of what college was going to be like by the way he dressed and conducted his classes. He always wore nice slacks and a shirt and tie. This was unusual because most other teachers dressed in a more casual way. He didn't assign any "busy work," he made assignments which helped us learn and understand, not feel as if we were wasting time. He made sure that we understood the material when we came to class the following day by welcoming questions on the assignment, at first, then giving a quiz on that material. This helped us learn, just as his lectures did.

Mr. Wilson's lectures were most interesting and informative. He really impressed us because he rarely referred to his book or notes. He always welcomed questions. If he didn't know the answer, which happened very rarely, he would find out by the next day. Also, he used examples in his lectures that related to our daily lives or added a touch of humor.

One of his major concerns was that of making sure that all of the students had developed a reasonable understanding of the material. If he felt that your grades or progress were below the average considerably or if you didn't feel comfortable with your work, he would stay after school to provide extra help.

Mr. Wilson realized that his love for physics was not shared by everyone, therefore, he set up experiments and arranged for speakers to come and talk about various science-related topics. He even arranged tours to Oakridge Nuclear Station. Occasionally, he would share his adventures of hiking through the mountains and keeping up his honeybee farm.

Aside from teaching physics, Mr. Wilson served somewhat as the school's electrician. Everytime a teacher had a problem with an overhead or filmstrip projector, tape recorder or television, he'd call Mr. Wilson to fix it.

Mr. Wilson was also the sponsor of the photography club. He trained members of the newspaper staff to take and develop their own pictures instead of hiring a photographer. He also learned to operate the computers so that his senior students could at least have the opportunity to gain a general idea of how to work them since a computer course was not offered in the regular curriculum.

Mr. Wilson is an effective teacher because he has earned the respect of the students and other teachers of Gaffney Senior High. He makes his classes interesting and informative and doesn't overemphasize grades. Most importantly he achieves the goal of being an effective teacher, having students learn.

I think this example illustrates that group work can yield impressive results. Obviously, it is an indirect illustration of the benefits of group work, but I would contend that this student reviewer demonstrates critical abilities developed by the group process. I chose this example because in it we see an average writer offering help to another average writer. I could have chosen drafts written by excellent writers. I have such examples, and, as one might expect, the changes from rough draft to final draft are often dramatic. But it is my experience that excellent writers come to our writing classes with the ability to revise. They often do produce remarkable revisions, but one often wonders just what role advice in the reviewing process plays in those revisions.

It is much more important for us to see what kinds of help average writers can give—and receive. Here an average writer has offered some very good advice. As an experienced teacher of writing, I could hardly offer better advice than the reviewer's suggestion that the writer develop her ideas more fully and provide the reader with more detail. Of course, one could argue that this advice is applicable in most situations and that the reviewer is simply parroting back what she has heard teachers say many times before. I do not think this is the case, however, because of the specific comments she makes about the writer's paragraphing. It is clear to me that the reviewer intuits a connection between these underdeveloped paragraphs and the overall lack of detail in this paper. In almost every case, her advice concerning weak paragraphing is right on target.

In addition, I am impressed by the questions the reviewer asks the writer. She goes beyond stylistic and mechanical matters to ask the writer just what she intends to say. I too wonder just why one needs to lecture on a topic to get students' respect. I also wonder how the students in this physics class were able to recognize that this teacher knew what he was doing.

These are certainly not earthshattering insights into this paper, but they surely helped the writer make the paper better. I am particularly impressed by the fact that these comments come from a student who began the course writing paragraphs marked by a lack of development and by a tendency toward vague statements like the ones she is questioning in this draft. By the end of this course, she had not completely solved these problems, but she was beginning to develop the critical eye which will help her write better.

One other factor in this student analysis is worth mentioning. The student reviewer was given no critique sheet in the process of producing this analysis. She was simply asked to write a letter showing how the essay could be improved. Her letter demonstrates that she has understood many of the principles introduced by critique sheets earlier.

But the final measure of success is the product at the end of the process, right? While I would not agree with this statement entirely, I do think that we can see important improvements from the rough draft to the final draft of this essay. The reviewer suggested that paragraphs three, four, and five in the rough draft were problematic. In looking back at paragraph three in that draft, we can see that the writer moves from a description of Mr. Wilson's entrance into the classroom to a general statement concerning what he did for the first week. As the reviewer suggests, there is also a problem in the connection between paragraphs three and four. The writer moves from a statement of what Mr. Wilson would do for the first week (at the end of paragraph three) back to the first day's class, in which Mr. Wilson expressed his objectives for the course (at the beginning of paragraph four). In the revised paper, paragraph two is given to a description of Mr. Wilson's behavior on the first day and of his method of stating course objectives and establishing rapport with the students. In the next paragraph, the writer moves to a general discussion of the students that Mr. Wilson taught and of the manner in which he conducted himself.

In general, the paragraphing is much improved in the final draft of this essay. But are all of the changes in the final draft good? Probably not. There are places where detail in the first draft is omitted in the second; for example, information concerning the way Mr. Wilson dealt with students who had not done their homework disappears. And does the writer remedy all of the problems her reviewer noted? Clearly, she does not. The reviewer suggests, for example, that the introduction is in need of some work; she asks for "something to catch the reader's attention more." One still feels this need after reading the introduction to the final draft.

This example, then, shows that peer review does not always produce perfect revisions. And, as noted early in this essay, there are many other potential problems for the teacher who would use peer critiques in her class. I have certainly not offered solutions to all of these problems here. Such solutions do not exist. But should that cause us to abandon group work?

Problems versus Benefits

Perhaps we can best answer this question by once again looking at the problems teachers fear and balancing them with the potential benefits of peer critiques. The following chart reveals some interesting relationships.

Fears	*Potential Benefits*
Students may plagiarize.	Students may share ideas.
Students may be overly harsh on the work of peers.	Students may develop the ability to see problems in peers' papers and their own.
Students may become domineering.	Students may develop leadership abilities.
Students may become lax.	Students may enjoy a non-threatening environment in which to write.
Students may be intimidated by the excellent work of their peers.	Students may benefit from seeing excellent work by their peers.
Students may become dependent upon help from peers.	Students may become more confident writers with help from their peers.

Each of the fears of group work is balanced by a corresponding potential benefit which might arise in the critiquing process. We should not allow such fears to cause us to avoid group work. To do so is to make our goal avoiding failure rather than achieving success.

Any teacher can make sure that nothing goes wrong. If he wants to make sure that there is no plagiarism, he can see to it that there is no sharing of ideas whatsoever and that all writing is done in class. If she wants to ensure that students do not dominate conversations, she can plan the class so that there is no student talk. If he fears that some students may take advantage of editing help from peers, he can strictly forbid students to share what they know with one another.

The teacher who uses peer critiques, on the other hand, cannot be motivated by fear of failure. Group critiques are not for teachers who spend a lot of time worrying about what might go wrong in the writing class: they are open invitations for things to go wrong. Paradoxically, they are also invitations for students to engage in real learning. For learning can take place only in those situations in which teachers and students do not know beforehand exactly what will take place in the classroom. Learning is always spontaneous; we never know exactly how it will happen or what shape it will assume.

From semester to semester, I never know exactly how group critiques will work; I never know what personalities will be in each group. I continue to use groups, however, because they allow me to teach writing as a process and because they allow students to become learners and teachers simultaneously.

The basic premise of group work seems contradictory to students and, I suspect, to many teachers. Students come to us to learn something about writing, but rather than offering them sage advice which will make them better writers, we ask them to become advisors to others who wish to become better writers and to learn from these same learners.

But this seeming contradiction becomes a paradox when we look more closely. All writers need to know how readers will react to what they have written—group work allows student writers to experience these reactions. However, one does not become a writer until she learns to trust her own instincts, to know that ultimately she, and she alone, is responsible for what is on the page. Group work helps the student writer move toward this responsibility, for it provides a reader whose role is to nudge, like an alter ego, rather than to negate, like a dictator.

APPENDIX
Critique Sheet for Transactional Essay

1. Is there one single point this paper is trying to make? Write a sentence which captures that point if there is. If there isn't, explain, as best you can, the confusion you feel.

2. Is the overall organization of this paper effective? What is the primary organizing device? Point to any places where the organization breaks down.

3. Does the paper contain information that will be interesting and/or useful to its designated audience? Point out any passages which contain information which might insult the reader's intelligence.

4. Does the introduction give the reader a clear idea of what the paper is about? Does it capture the reader's attention? Does it avoid trite generalizations and stage directions? Does it contain a thesis or center of gravity? Try to think of one other way in which the writer could have begun this paper.

5. Does the conclusion work? Is it basically a summary? Does it suggest a plan of action? Does it do something else? What? Try to offer the writer one other way to conclude the essay.

6. Paragraph checklist:

   a. Give the number of any paragraph that lacks unity or coherence. Explain.

   b. Give the number of any paragraph that lacks development. What is missing?

   c. Give the number of any paragraph that seems to be out of place in the essay. Where should it go? Why?

   d. Give the number of any paragraph that lacks transition.

7. Word choice checklist:

   a. List any trite or clichéd words.

   b. List any words that sound pompous or overly formal.

Making Assignments, Judging Writing, and Annotating Papers: Some Suggestions

Richard L. Larson
Herbert H. Lehman College, City University of New York

Whether or not they follow a syllabus prepared by the head of the writing program or by a departmental committee, or develop their own assignments, or do some of both, new teachers are usually responsible for three of the central acts performed by any teacher of writing: giving students their assignments (or invitations) for writing, making judgments about students' writing (whether in the form of grades, advice about revision, or summary analyses), and offering comments about students' papers. I offer here some suggestions to new teachers about how they might perform each of these acts.

Writing Assignments

Assignments not only tell the students what they are expected to write about, they define (taken as a group) the emphases and structure of the course, and signal some of the values held by the teacher. Furthermore, if the assignments are written out, they act as examples of the teacher's own writing. So the instructions should be as thoughtfully prepared and as precisely expressed as possible. A poor assignment, or a potentially good assignment poorly described, is always an invitation to weak papers from students. What follows is a list of questions that a teacher might consider for each writing assignment before distributing it. Considering these questions before giving out an assignment will not guarantee the effectiveness of the assignment, but doing so may enable the teacher to improve the assignment and to avoid common causes of weak papers.

Writing Assignments: Questions to Consider

1. Is the task the students must accomplish clearly defined? That is, can they see exactly what task they are called upon to perform in writing (e.g., to identify the traits of a literary character, to report

the results of a survey or experiment, to propose a plan of action to meet a need, to elucidate some complex terminology, to explain some personal feelings about a situation)? Will they have a clear idea of what the paper they are to produce should do?

2. Have you a clear idea about what a desirable response to the assignment might look like? Should you share any features of this desirable response with the students? Are the bases for evaluation of their papers clear to students?

3. If appropriate, are the students given a clear idea of what steps or cognitive/conceptual activities they will need to undertake in writing the paper? If, for instance, the citation of certain kinds of data in support of a conclusion is required, can the students determine that such citations are required? (It is possible, of course, that some requirements will have been established in earlier assignments. But if such requirements have not been established, they should be made clear as the assignment under consideration is made.)

4. Can the assignment be completed with some success by students at different levels of ability? If not, is the limitation on how many students can do the assignment important?

5. Does the assignment demand of the students some exercise of judgment, some engagement with—resolution of—a problem? (Assignments that can be answered *yes* or *no* with little explanation, or that demand no more than a list of items, may present no challenge to the students and give them no practice in thinking out a response.)

6. Is it clear why students are asked to write this paper, that is, is it clear how the writing is related to the overall plan for the course?

7. Is the assignment likely to be of interest to the students? Is doing it likely to lead to some learning (some understandings, some conclusions) about the subject—to some recognitions that the students did not have before doing the assignment? Do the students, that is, stand to gain from the assignment something more than just another completed paper?

8. Does the assignment help the students envisage a credible writing situation—an honest purpose and an interested, responsive audience?

Judgments

Teachers ought not to view a piece of writing as a collection of separate parts (even if the essay impresses them as exactly that); they should view a piece of writing as a whole, as an act of communication undertaken by one human being for one or more others. That is to say, a piece of writing, or a spoken utterance, is an action taken in order to reach an audience; it should be judged as a total action. Difficulties with syntax, spelling, transitions, the shapes of paragraphs, and so on should be judged in perspective; the teacher might ask how these weaknesses or these difficulties affect the overall success of the author in completing the act of communication that he or she has attempted. As a reader, do I respond to this piece as the author evidently wished me to respond? Why or why not? The following questions may help teaching assistants to approach papers in this spirit, and to judge them accordingly.

Some Questions for Use in Judging a Piece of Writing

1. If the assignment that evoked the writing gives specific directions, does the writing carry out those directions?

2. What are the special characteristics (e.g., citation of certain kinds of information, inclusion of particular kinds of details, demonstration that the writer is aware of any special interests operating among members of the audience, and so on) that a paper must exhibit in order to complete the assigned task successfully? Does the essay have these features?

3. At or close to the beginning, is the author's purpose in the paper clear? Is it clear why the author comes before the reader at this time, on this subject? Is there a focus for the essay? Is it clear what problems, if any, the author is addressing? Is it clear what rhetorical or cognitive acts the author intends to complete during the paper?

4. During the paper, does the author make clear how all parts of the essay relate to the carrying out of his or her purpose, i.e., to the accomplishment of the "action" promised? If the author's purpose changes, is there an explanation of the change?

5. Is an overall plan for the whole essay evident? Is a plan evident within individual sections? Is the plan suitable to the author's purpose?

6. Is the essay as a whole coherent, that is, does the sequence of steps taken by the author in the essay remain clear, and can the reader follow the author's plan?

7. Is the essay correct in its facts?

8. Are the data cited adequate to the author's purpose? Are important data omitted or neglected?

9. Where data are interpreted, are the interpretations fair and reasonable?

10. Has the author taken care to explain important assumptions made during the paper?

11. Has the author recognized important implications of the data cited or inferences drawn?

12. Does the author avoid including data not related to his or her purpose?

13. Is the author's reasoning sound? If particular data are applied to generalizations in order to reach a conclusion, is the process followed sound?

14. At the end, has the author completed the action he or she promised? Has the author accomplished the essay's purpose? Has he or she solved (or offered a reasonable proposed solution to) the problem raised at the start?

15. Does the author's conclusion build upon, and take account of, data and reasoning in the body of the paper?

16. Is the style reasonably clear, free of distracting errors in punctuation and of syntactic features that complicate reading?

17. Does the author earn the reader's respect for his or her views?

Comments

New teachers are almost always responsible for commenting on or annotating students' papers. Sometimes they comment orally, in conferences or even in small groups or workshops. More often, they comment in writing. What follows is a group of suggestions about making written comments (though I think the same suggestions would apply to comments made in a conference, small group, or workshop). Following these suggestions, of course, will not ensure that the teacher's comments are incisive or that they highlight the same features of a paper that another teacher might highlight. But the suggestions will help teachers prepare comments that enable students to learn, and that—perhaps as important—give students the sense that their papers have been read by thoughtful human beings who genuinely want to help them communicate their ideas more completely and effectively.

These suggestions assume that comments on students' papers should have three purposes: (1) to identify the paper's strong points as well as points in need of improvement, (2) to suggest how the student might prepare a more effective paper next time, and (3) to give the student some explanation of why the instructor reached a particular evaluation of the paper.

The suggestions also assume that an effective comment on an essay can be a powerful teaching instrument—often more influential on the student's writing than class discussions of sample papers. The comment, after all, expresses what the teacher values in writing and locates places where the student has reached those values and where the student needs to do additional work in order to reach those values. In the writing of comments, the suggestions assert, it is better to explain a criticism or proposed revision with excessive thoroughness than to offer it so sketchily that the student cannot learn from it.

Writing Comments on Students' Essays

Marginal Comments

In making marginal comments, remember that you are neither a proofreader (responsible for normalizing spelling, punctuation, and typographical style) nor an editor (responsible for improving diction, idiom, and possibly syntax) nor a judge (responsible for rendering a verdict of "good" or "bad"), but a teacher from whom students hope to get help in improving their reasoning, organization, style, and so on. If your students are to learn from what you write in the margins of their papers, your observations must be clear and self-explanatory.

1. Use marginal comments primarily to call attention to some particular strength or weakness in the paper—usually a strength or weakness of detail, or at any rate one that can be located precisely—at the point where it occurs. Usually comments that refer to the reasoning or design or style of the whole essay are better reserved for the general (final) comment.

2. Feel free to ask questions about points that the student makes, to ask for clarification, to point out (where such a comment seems appropriate) other possible views of the subject. Let the student know that you are interested in what he or she has to say to you.

3. Avoid using "?" and terse queries like "What?" or "How come?" or "So what?" If you feel that the student's reasoning is unsatisfactory (e.g., because pertinent data are omitted or because an unsound conclusion has been drawn or because the significance of an idea is not made clear), explain your judgment precisely enough to let the student know where you think his or her thinking is faulty. Do not leave the student guessing that your notation simply reveals a

difference of opinion between the two of you, or believing that your opinions on the point in question are unjustifiably rigid. Better fewer marginal comments well explained than a large number of cryptic, uninformative jottings.

4. In general, avoid arguing with the student. Focus on passages in which the student might demonstrably have improved what he or she has done. If the matter on which you are tempted to comment is simply a source of disagreement between the two of you on a point where reasonable people might differ, omit the comment. Avoid asking a student to "explain" a point on which his or her reasoning is fairly obvious or self-evident. Ask for explanation only when the reasoning is in fact hidden and needs to be disclosed. Try not to quibble over matters of diction and sentence structure that reflect only differences between your taste and that of the student. Comment on style only when you can propose a visible improvement over the student's way of expressing an idea.

5. Do not hesitate to note places where the student's thinking is especially effective, his or her style especially pleasing, his or her organization notably well planned, and so on.

General (Final) Comments

The purpose of the general comments is to record your overall impression of the paper and, more important, to point out goals for the writer to seek in revising that paper or in writing his or her next paper. Most comments should not be merely judgments about the paper at hand, although, of course, some comments that analyze a paper in detail can imply constructive suggestions for revision or for the elimination of recurrent weaknesses in the student's writing. The list that follows sums up the characteristics a good general comment may have; it is not a list of items to be included in every general comment you write.

1. Unless the mechanics and syntax are hopelessly inept (sometimes, to be sure, they are), make the general comment more than a list or summary of such errors. Play down mechanical difficulties where possible.

2. Show respect for the student's paper; recognize that it is the student's work—the student's property. Try not to treat it as if the student were doing something for you. Try not to treat the paper as if the principal difficulty were that the student did not do what you wanted him or her to do or what you thought he or she ought to do. Work, if possible, from the student's perspective as well as

from your own. Leave the student believing, after reading your comment, that the essay still belongs to him or her and that you are out to help the student to do better what he or she wanted to do— or to help the student improve his or her choice of subject or perspective or emphasis so that he or she can earn the reader's respect more successfully.

3. Point out strengths or good features of the essay wherever you can, rather than focusing exclusively on weaknesses. (This suggestion does not imply, however, that you should pore over a bad paper in search of a trifling virtue on which to comment.) If the paper marks an improvement over the student's earlier work, say so and tell why you think so.

4. In part, at least, let your general comments inform the student how well he or she met the problems posed by the assignment. Deal with this point even if you plan to devote most of the comment to matters not related to the student's handling of the specific assignment.

5. Concentrate on the most important difficulties of substance, structure, and style that affect the paper as a whole. If the reason for criticism of some features of the paper is not obvious, suggest why these features are indeed weaknesses and, where possible, propose changes that would have improved the paper. Be sure that the student can see why you think he or she should have done things differently; make clear how the proposed changes would improve the paper. Such comments are especially important if you ask your students to revise their papers. Specify in the comment what the student's principal aims should be in revising.

6. Try to see that the comment is constructive—that it has "transfer value." That is, try to help students to improve their work on future papers. To achieve this purpose, search out fundamental features that may be in need of improvement: factual inaccuracies, unclear assertions, lack of coherence between sentences and paragraphs, reliance on unrecognized and undefended assumptions, excessively abstract diction, unsound generalizations or conclusions based on inadequate evidence, and so on. Describe and illustrate these features so that students will understand them and can learn to recognize them as they revise rough drafts of future papers. Call particular attention, if possible, to difficulties that recur in successive essays by the same student.

7. Let your general comment support, and be supported by, the marginal comments; the two sets of observations should work together. Often you will be able to illustrate comments on the paper by re-

ferring to difficulties pointed out in detail in marginalia. But the general comment should not be merely a disjointed summary or repetition of the marginal comments. It must bring your separate responses to the paper into focus; it must give the student a coherent assessment of the paper as a whole.

8. Unless you have developed a special relationship with the student in which irony will not be misinterpreted, take care that your comments are not ironic, sarcastic, condescending, or inclined to belittle the student as a person. Irony can only anger students; it does not instruct them. Slangy, flippant admonitions (e.g., "Don't slit your wrists over this grade") should be avoided; a teacher should give more thoughtful and beneficial advice.

9. Focus your comment on the paper, not on the personality or motivation of its author. Even making assumptions about what led the writer to adopt a particular attitude or discuss a specific subject is usually unwise. Of course, if parts of a paper are ambiguous or if the emphasis is fuzzy, you can and should ask the writer which of two or three possible meanings he or she intended to convey, or whether you are correct in believing that the writer meant to emphasize a particular point.

   Finally, one implication in point 4 above bears repeating: comments on students' papers should bear some relationship to what the student was asked to accomplish in the essay. As has been suggested earlier, it is wise to anticipate, when planning an assignment, the features that will result in success or failure in students' work, and perhaps to anticipate the kinds of comments one might need to make on that work. Such advance planning may help strengthen the assignment; it may also simplify and accelerate the process of responding to students' work.

I hope that following these three sets of suggestions will help instructors work more successfully at the point where, finally, the real teaching of writing occurs: at the point where the instructor evokes and responds to students' writing. Students learn to write by writing; the teacher best fulfills his or her professional responsibility by helping to ensure that students are encouraged and guided toward their best writing.

On Not Being a Composition Slave

Maxine Hairston
University of Texas at Austin

The Conventional Wisdom about Paper Grading

Until very recently, most college composition teachers have not known what they were doing. That is not an accusation; it is simply a fact. We have had no research that would allow us to compare one method of teaching with another, and we have had no evaluation instruments to measure the effectiveness of either teachers or theories. Few college writing teachers have been really trained; rather they have learned their craft, if they have learned it at all, through apprenticeships, brownbag seminars, or short orientation sessions at the beginning of the semester. Mostly, however, they have operated almost entirely from a body of conventional wisdom that is held *a priori* by both seasoned and new instructors, and is reinforced by corridor conversation and office bull sessions.

According to that conventional wisdom, to be a good composition teacher one must do two things: first, one must mark all student papers meticulously and comment on them copiously; second, one must hold one-to-one student conferences regularly (two a semester is the minimum, once a week is much better). The assumption that underlies this doctrine is that students' writing will improve in direct proportion to the amount of time their teachers spend on their papers.

Now this is a seductive doctrine. It has a kind of logical appeal that says if people are shown their mistakes, they will stop making them. It can also make teachers feel good, for at least in passing back a paper covered with red[1] they are demonstrating that they know all the rules and have not let one lapse slip by. It also gives the people who are supervising new teachers a tangible basis for judging their performance. It is simple: the more marks on the students' papers, the better the teacher.

Unfortunately, there are also serious drawbacks to this approach to teaching writing. First, it is a totally impractical model for most writing

teachers in most writing programs, and, if held up as an ideal, will almost certainly damage the writing program in important ways. Second,
most of the time this error-focused method of teaching writing does not
work, and for good psychological and behavioral reasons.

The Effect on Teachers

Let us look first at what happens to writing teachers who try to perform
conscientiously in a system that stresses heavy grading and frequent
conferences. First, if they are teaching even two sections of writing, they
quickly become overwhelmed by the grading burden, become slaves, in
short. To grade the paper of the average writer thoroughly, including
positive as well as negative comments, takes at least thirty minutes—
frequently more. Two sections, forty-eight students—twenty-four hours
of grading for every set of papers. Add time for class preparation,
classes, office hours, and conferences, and the workload for half-time
teaching jumps to at least forty hours every time a set of papers comes
in. I have known more than one faculty member to spend almost that
much on just *one* composition class.

Now, teachers who spend this much time on their composition teaching may well get good results and see improvement in their students'
writing by the end of the term, but I think they would be hard-pressed
to prove that the improvement occurred *because* of their grading and
frequent conferences. Rather, the students may have bloomed and
worked hard because they realized the teacher was investing a great deal
in the class. Like all people, they respond to attention and try to please
the person who lavishes it on them, particularly if that attention is be-
nevolent. Usually this kind of teacher also gets good teaching evaluations
that reinforce his or her conviction that intensive composition teaching
is the only kind that works.

It does not take long, however, for most faculty and graduate students
to realize that this kind of composition teaching will exhaust them and
that they will get almost nothing else done if they keep it up. When that
truth strikes them, faculty respond in several ways. Those with strong
survival instincts escape in any way they can and teach as little composition as possible, all the while proclaiming—and often quite honestly—
that they really like to teach writing but cannot afford to do it. Others,
less fortunate or less assertive, continue to teach writing regularly but
do not give it as much time as they think they should and consequently
feel guilty and, finally, resentful. Inevitably students sense that
resentment.

Another group of faculty doggedly persist in trying to meet the ideal by painstakingly grading every error on every paper and writing extensive marginal and end comments. Teachers who do try to meet this traditional standard become the departmental drudges, who spend so much of their time on their teaching that they have no time for those other, more prestigious professional activities that pay off in promotions and raises. So they go unrewarded by the academic system, and they take on the role of the faculty martyrs—overworked, underpaid, and unappreciated. They justify their failure to do any writing themselves by saying they are devoting all their time to their students, but often they also end up disillusioned with the students who do not seem to be taking their advice to heart. They suspect that too often students don't even read their comments, but look only at the grade.

It all has a familiar ring. "I work my fingers to the bone, and nobody appreciates it." "After all I've done for you, how can you treat me this way?" And indeed there are distressing parallels between self-sacrificing parents who feel used and neglected by their families and self-sacrificing composition teachers who feel exploited and ignored by their students and their departments. Both feel they are trapped doing the dirty work while others get the glory. That kind of self-pity does not make good parents *or* good teachers.

But probably this intensive model for marking compositions works the greatest hardship on the graduate student teachers. If they accept the doctrine that they must mark every error on a paper, make comments that show the students how to improve, and then have them revise their papers, they will either invest far more time than they can afford on student papers, or they will constantly feel guilty because they are not doing their job right. Chances are that they will err on the side of too much grading because reading a text closely and criticizing it is what they do best. It is also easier than writing their own papers, and it brings approval from supervising professors. Unfortunately, consistently spending thirty to forty minutes on each student paper can also terminate a graduate career if the graduate student begins to take incompletes in his or her own courses.

The Effect on Students

But all the drudgery and sacrifice on the part of writing teachers might be justified if it helped students to learn to write; unfortunately, we have no evidence that it does. In a recent essay in *Freshman English News*, C. H. Knoblauch and Lil Brannon of New York University summarized the research that has been done on how students respond to corrections and comments on their writing.[2] They cite the summary of one study as representative of all the research findings:

> Different types of teacher comments on student themes have equally small influences on student writing. . . . Either students do not read the comments or they read them and do not attempt to implement suggestions and correct errors.[3]

The conclusion of another study was even more discouraging:

> [King] found that students rarely understood directly corrective commentary and that even when they did understand comments in the other two categories [identifying errors and citing rules] they were not necessarily aided by either. . . . The implications of her research, to the extent that they can be generalized, are as plain as they are troubling.
>
> (1) Students often do not comprehend teacher responses to their writing; (2) even when they do, they do not always use those responses and may not know how to use them; (3) when they use them, they do not necessarily write more effectively as a result.[4]

Knoblauch and Brannon do not conclude from their study that teacher comments on papers are useless; rather they conclude that the traditional kinds of comments do not do what teachers think they do. More on that shortly.

But why have these traditional methods not worked? Well, if we use a little common sense about learning theory and remember some basic precepts of humanistic psychology, it is not hard to see why the copious and detailed comments of the instructor often fail to make an impression on the student.

First, numerous corrections combined with long marginal and end comments produce cognitive overload. The student simply cannot process and absorb the amount of information he or she is getting, much less adequately respond to it. Often the student does not understand the teacher's terminology or cannot recognize the errors identified.

Second, when the teacher marks every mistake in a paper—and often, to the student's confusion, teachers cannot agree on what constitute mistakes—he or she presents the students with so many remedial tasks that many students give up because there seems to be no possibility of success. Such a teacher has violated the behavioral principle that people master skills and solve large problems by tackling small, manageable tasks a few at a time. Good coaches and counselors set limited objectives for their clients.

Third, as Carl Rogers points out in his essay on communication, most people protect their egos from negative and threatening messages by throwing up defensive barriers and refusing to acknowledge the messages.[5] In the same way, many students will react to a mass of negative criticism by refusing to read it. A heavily marked paper with a low grade is so intimidating that, as R. Baird Shuman says, "any psychologically healthy student survives by pretending that it doesn't matter and by showing the contempt that will support this pretense."[6]

Fourth, most students do not know how to use their teacher's comments to improve their writing. As Nancy Sommers and other researchers have shown, novice writers have little concept of what it means to make substantive revisions in their writings.[7] Rather they focus on surface-level, single-word changes and resist making changes that involve major reorganization or actual rewriting. I think the truth is that as writing teachers we have expected students to revise their work, but we have not really taught them how to go about it. Moreover, as Mina Shaughnessy points out in *Errors and Expectations,* once students have written a paper and turned it in for a grade they regard their task as completed, and they are not interested in working on it again.[8] Under such circumstances, extensive comments on a paper may really be unwelcome and thus ignored if possible.

Fifth, students may resist reading comments because they get mixed signals from them. Research now going on at New York University and reported by Nancy Sommers at the 1981 convention of the Conference on College Composition and Communication indicates that teachers often give contradictory advice in their marginal comments. For example, a teacher may suggest to a student that he or she eliminate a paragraph but at the same time point out needed corrections within the paragraph. And when students begin to get confused as they read teachers' comments, many of them will simply quit.

Finally, teachers who habitually try to mark every error in a paper, no matter what the cost to themselves, may wind up unintentionally giving their students two very negative messages: first, that they really do not care what students say, they care only that they say it correctly; and second, that they consider teaching writing a great burden and a thankless task. Those powerful indirect messages can effectively cancel out the direct ones in which the teacher has invested so much time.

Sooner or later, then, most teachers who try to handle today's students and today's teaching loads by using the traditional product-centered method of teaching writing are going to burn out. They are trying to teach writing by acting as editors and critics for writers who are not far enough advanced to profit by the kind of help their teachers are offering them. Most students cannot absorb such advice, much less act on it. Teachers who persist in this no-win situation either will become moles who do nothing but grade papers and complain or will become cynical and stop trying to help students at all. Either choice is an admission of failure.

What Are the Alternatives?

How can writing teachers emancipate themselves from the drudgery of grading and learn to evaluate students' papers quickly and efficiently, but also responsibly and constructively? I think first we have to change our attitudes about error and, if possible, our students' attitudes toward us as error hunters. As Lee Odell has put it, most people think of English teachers as they do of policemen—people who lurk in the shadows waiting for people to make mistakes so they can punish them for it. Too often that image of us is accurate when we are grading papers. Instead of reading to find out what a student has to say, we read with error at the fronts of our minds, our pencils ready to tag all lapses from the code. It is a deadly practice that will kill whatever pleasure we might get from a paper.

So take the first step to liberate yourself by sitting on your hands and not even thinking about marking errors on a paper until you have read it through. You will not notice nearly as many mistakes the second time. And when you convince students that your first concern is *what* they say, you may give them the incentive to gamble a little and write something ambitious without worrying first about spelling and punctuation. None of us can grow as writers unless we take risks, but student writers will take as few risks as possible if they think their teachers are just waiting to pounce on their mistakes.

Second, create a positive, supportive environment in the writing classroom. Show that you care tremendously about whether your students learn to write. Encourage them to keep journals and do free-writing on their own. Demonstrate to your students that you too are a writer by sharing your own writing with the class. Duplicate good student papers and analyze them with your students to show them that writing is a way of learning and growing and of increasing their control over their own lives.

Third, show your students how the writing process works, guiding them through several drafts of a paper and emphasizing the generative and tentative nature of the process. During the drafting stage, follow Donald Murray's advice to act as a diagnostician and a coach, not a judge.[9] Try to make nonthreatening, facilitative comments that show writers what changes they could make to improve their writing. Diagnose the chief problem each writer may be having but do not focus on specific errors.

Fourth, arrange for your students to help each other as much as possible by setting up groups in which they work together to generate ideas, plan their papers, and do guided reviews of each other's papers while they are in the draft state. You can shift much of the burden for the practical evaluation of writing—that is, asking whether it works with the audience for which it is intended—to student review sessions. Once students have been shown how to read and critique a paper constructively, they can do a great deal for each other. Moreover, their own writing improves as they help each other.

Fifth, set priorities about errors. Decide which are the most potentially damaging to student writing and focus on those, spending some class time working from students' own writing. Decide to mark only a limited number of errors in any paper but stress that students are still responsible for trying to reduce errors in all their writing. Remind them that you are not a copy editor; you are a writing coach. Do not rewrite their papers for them.

Sixth, turn your class into a writing lab at regular intervals and have the students work on their papers when you are there to help them. You can also have them exchange papers and help each other at this stage— professional writers get help from their peers, and there is no reason why student writers should be denied that option. Also give students time in class to edit their own papers when they get a draft back from you or their fellow students.

Seventh, spend class time teaching students how to revise. Analyze problem paragraphs in class, explaining the terms you use to identify places that need revising. Then have everyone—including yourself— rewrite the paragraph and analyze and discuss the rewritten versions. And when you mark papers, think about how students can use your comments to improve their writing.

Eighth, seek specific advice about grading from two excellent books: Donald Murray's *A Writer Teaches Writing* (Boston: Houghton Mifflin, 1968) and *How to Handle the Paper Load* (Urbana, Illinois: National Council of Teachers of English, 1979).

Ninth, try to limit your grading to marking a few important errors, noting several things that the student has done well, and suggesting one major change the student could make that would improve his or her writing. And if you are really pressed for time, remember that you do not have to read everything that students write. Your final goal is to teach them to become their own critics and editors. You can push them toward that goal by showing them how to take responsibility for their own growth as writers, and by putting them on their own at least part of the time. You do your part by creating a congenial atmosphere in which to write.

We all know that students must have instruction in writing and feedback on their writing in order to become better writers. What little research we have certainly supports that conclusion.[10] But we must focus on ways to give them quality instruction and quality feedback rather than overwhelming them with more advice than they can absorb and more criticism than they can tolerate. We need to realize that there is not necessarily a positive correlation between our success as writing teachers and the amount of time we spend grading our papers. What we do with students in class before they write and as they write may help them far more than any number of comments after the fact. And creating a positive environment that makes them want to write may turn out to be the most important thing we ever do for them. But slaves have a hard time projecting a positive outlook. That is a good reason not to be one.

Notes

1. See Donald Murray, *A Writer Teaches Writing* (Boston: Houghton Mifflin, 1968), 19.

2. C. H. Knoblauch and Lil Brannon, "Teacher Commentary on Student Writing: The State of the Art," *Freshman English News* 10, no. 2 (Fall 1981): 1–3.

3. R. J. Marzano and S. Arthur, "Teacher Comments on Student Essays: It Doesn't Matter What You Say," University of Colorado, Denver, 1977 (ERIC, ED 147864), quoted in Knoblauch and Brannon.

4. Cited by Marzano and Arthur, in Knoblauch and Brannon.

5. Carl Rogers, "Communication: Its Blocking and Its Facilitation," in *On Becoming a Person* (Boston: Houghton Mifflin, 1970), 329–37.

6. R. Baird Shuman, "How to Grade Student Writing," in *Classroom Practices in Teaching English, 1979–80: How to Handle the Paper Load*, ed. Gene Stanford (Urbana, Ill.: National Council of Teachers of English, 1979), 95.

7. Nancy Sommers, "Revision Strategies of Student Writers and Experienced Adult Writers," *College Composition and Communication* 31, no. 4 (Dec. 1980): 378.

8. Mina Shaughnessy, *Errors and Expectations: A Guide for the Teacher of Basic Writing* (New York: Oxford Univ. Press, 1977), 79.

9. Murray, 19.

10. See Betty Bamberg, "Composition Instruction Does Make a Difference: A Comparison of the High School Preparation of College Freshmen in Regular and Remedial English Classes," *Research in the Teaching of English* 12, no. 1 (Feb. 1978): 47–59; Knoblauch and Brannon.

Portfolio Evaluation:
Room to Breathe and Grow

Christopher C. Burnham
New Mexico State University

Reviewing more than twenty-five years of research examining the effects of teachers' comments on student writing, C. H. Knoblauch and Lil Brannon draw three conclusions. First, students generally do not comprehend written teacher responses. Second, when students do comprehend the comments, they generally do not know how to use them. And third, when students do use the comments, they do not necessarily produce more effective writing.[1] Similarly, Nancy Sommers examines marginal notations on freshman compositions and concludes that "most teachers' comments are not text-specific and could be interchanged, rubber-stamped, from text to text."[2] The comments may notify a student of a problem in the text, but they help the student neither to understand the problem nor to solve it. These studies and others illustrate the difficulties teachers have responding effectively to student writing.

While researchers are offering these less-than-comforting observations, response and evaluation remain major concerns of inexperienced teachers. Recently, at a workshop for our composition staff, I described the research presented above. Evaluations from that workshop indicated that most of the staff felt the workshop was not helpful but confusing. Presented with research that offers many questions but few answers, teachers felt unready to address the issues on their own. They preferred to continue their present practice even if it accomplished little. If I did not know that their practice was based on process consciousness and multiple drafting, conferences and individualized support for students as learners, I would be dismayed. Given the context, however, I considered the staff's reaction a normal one.

If response and evaluation are major sources of concern, even anxiety, among inexperienced teachers, just as important are the effects our response and evaluation have on writers. The anxiety and insecurity of many freshman writers can be traced directly to hostile or puzzling commentary from previous teachers. In addition, grading is an obsession with some students and can become a major block in the working rela-

125

tionship between student and teacher. What instructor has not been accused of subjectivity and arbitrariness? And how many, even while explaining their practice, have never suspected that the student's claim is at least partly justified? Although the real benefit a writing course offers students is their increased skill as writers and thinkers, their immediate concern, a legitimate one, is the grades they will receive. Anything that can mitigate their sensitivity to grades, anything that helps keep the channels of instruction between students and teachers open, should improve the teaching and learning of writing.

Given the complex problem of response and evaluation, trainers of teachers must give them all the helpful information available, while providing a buffer period during which inexperienced teachers can assimilate that information and practice responding and evaluating. Inexperienced teachers need time to develop their own philosophies of response and evaluation.

Some composition programs use internships or mentor systems to allow new teachers some experience while exempting them from complete responsibility. Others use group evaluation procedures in which instructors are not individually responsible for grading their students.[3] We have developed an alternative procedure that allows instructors the room they need to develop a philosophy and implement it while reserving to them the responsibility for grading. The procedure, portfolio evaluation, incorporates what we know about how students develop as writers by emphasizing process, multiple drafting, and collaborative learning. In addition, portfolio evaluation encourages instructors to become respondents to student writing rather than error-seeking proofreaders. Moreover, portfolio evaluation requires the careful planning and execution not only of the individual course but also of a training program to support teachers using the system, thereby encouraging staff development. Benefits accrue to individual instructors, the students they teach, and the program they teach in.

Overview

Briefly described, portfolio evaluation works like this. At specific points during the semester, students submit "finished drafts" of papers developed in class workshops. Instructors respond to these drafts not to provide an evaluation with a grade but to provide suggestions for revision as well as some general commentary about the individual's development as a writer. Instructors either accept the finished draft or turn it back for revision. The paper is accepted when the instructor considers the student to have met the specific minimum requirements for that assignment (e.g., the writer is using transitions to show coherence or the writer defends a clear thesis) and the writer is ready to tackle the next assignment in the sequence. When the paper is returned for revision, the instructor offers the feedback that will allow for effective revision. The "revise" notation provides the writer with another opportunity to succeed.

After successfully completing a predetermined number of the semester's assignments, the student can elect to compile a portfolio for final evaluation. Without a portfolio the student receives a C for the course. Students who have not completed the minimum number of finished drafts fail the course.

Qualified students who elect to compile a portfolio and compete for grades higher than C follow this procedure: First, they gather all the work they have done during the semester, review it, and choose examples of their best writing, which can include free-writing, journal writing, or narratives and poems. Then they write short explanations pointing to the features that make the writing good. These explanations show the criteria that students have developed through the semester to evaluate writing, and require students to make explicit criteria that have been implicit so far.

Second, students choose two previously submitted and approved drafts and revise them substantially in the light of all they have learned about writing during the semester. The students attach the original drafts to the revised papers so the instructor can see the changes the writers have made and the effect these revisions have had.

Third, using the material in the portfolio and their performance in class as "data," students write a short argumentative paper directed to the instructor, asserting that they have earned a particular grade and defending this assertion. Students submit the portfolios to the instructor, who evaluates them and informs students of the success of their portfolios during individual conferences at semester's end.

Preparation

The portfolio submitted for final evaluation represents the culmination of the semester's labor, and since so much depends on it the portfolio evaluation procedure must be carefully planned for both instructors and students. For instructors, the work begins before the semester, in a workshop designed to provide information about student writing and practice in responding to and evaluating it, as well as guidance in constructing a comprehensive syllabus for the course. In line with our program's insistence that individual instructors maintain complete responsibility for the sections they teach, we do not have a common syllabus for freshman composition. Rather, we have a comprehensive list of departmentally approved goals and objectives for the course that all instructors use while planning and teaching their individual sections. These goals and objectives include the conventions of standard edited English, the structure and development of paragraphs and papers, various research techniques, a familiarity with the various purposes of writing (including the relation between writing and self-development), and collaborative learning procedures. These are the skills and concepts we have determined students should command when they leave freshman composition. In addition, TAs and new part-time staff use common textbooks that reflect the department's goals and objectives. The training program is keyed to and supports the use of these texts. We believe that making instructors responsible for their own sections makes them more demanding of themselves and in turn more demanding of their students. Ultimately, these increased demands enrich the entire program and the university.

The workshop before the semester begins considers five topics. First we discuss what kinds of response and evaluation frustrate student growth and what kinds encourage growth. We use a Shaughnessy error analysis approach, illustrating that grammar, if it is to be taught effectively, must be taught in the context of the students' own writing. By the end of this part of the workshop inexperienced instructors can note error patterns, focus on those where their efforts have the greatest chance of being effective, and develop instruction that will help students overcome problems.

The second aspect of the workshop is practice in actual responses to papers. Our efforts here focus on developing responses that will result in effective revision. We discuss the benefits of offering positive reinforcement and individualizing summary comments. We respond to a sample paper and critique our responses. We try to look at commentary as an instrument of change rather than evaluation. During the workshop we emphasize that there is no single way to respond effectively, and that principles can guide us but the real test is developing our own ways of responding to individual student needs and strengths.

Third, we spend time discussing and demonstrating workshop and one-on-one conference techniques that can be used to solve problems that might arise once papers are returned. Ideally, each paper should be returned at a short conference during which the instructor checks to make sure the student understands and can act upon the comments that have been made.

Our fourth concern is with ranges of acceptable performance, that is, with standards. Most of our freshman composition instructors have taught in our Basic Writing program, which uses a holistically scored common writing sample at exit. Therefore, our instructors know the procedure for holistic scoring and how to sort and rank papers. They are also aware of the exit criteria for Basic Writing, which in turn become the entrance-level expectations for regular freshman composition. In the workshop, we supply and discuss benchmark papers that illustrate general ranges of acceptable performance. The benchmarks represent ranges of performance rather than specific grades because the grade finally will result from performance in the portfolio rather than on any one assignment. This information gives instructors a sense of the program's standards, permitting them to make informed decisions regarding the acceptability of the finished drafts students submit along the way.

The fifth and final topic is the construction of the course syllabus. Any instructor who will be using the portfolio evaluation procedure must make that clear on his or her syllabus. First, instructors must outline the course requirements in terms of pass/fail. For example, during a fifteen-week semester, students will attempt nine formal assignments. To earn a C and qualify to submit a portfolio, students must complete seven assignments successfully, in addition, of course, to regular attendance and participation in class activities. After listing these minimum requirements, we include the announcement that grades higher than C will be awarded only to those submitting portfolios during the last weeks of class. Although showing such concern for final evaluation so early in the course seems contrary to the objectives of portfolio evaluation, it is the best means of informing students that they will be experiencing an unfamiliar method. Our concern is that the portfolio requirement be clear, and students properly forewarned.

After discussing how to announce the portfolio evaluation on the course syllabus, we spend time generating and responding to the myriad questions students will ask. Instructors must first make the point that the portfolio procedure is designed to benefit the student by taking advantage of the process through which students develop as writers. Since the process is gradual and often unpredictable, with quantum leaps occurring generally late in the semester, revising papers at the end of the course and submitting a portfolio allows students to show the instructor how much they ultimately learned, which is generally much more than the sum of their performances on individual assignments. During the practice question-and-answer session we emphasize that instructors must make clear to students how the "acceptable"/"revise" system will work and the different ways of completing the course. Students must also be warned of the dangers of missing work or falling behind with revisions since the assignments near the end of the course are more demanding than the earlier ones.

Instructors must also announce as a policy that if a paper is not accepted but turned back for revision, it must be revised and resubmitted before the next assignment is due. This policy assures the integrity of the developmental sequence of assignments in the course. Students need to understand that assignment 3 teaches skills needed for successful completion of assignment 4. Just as important, such a revision policy prevents abuses of the system. Inexperienced instructors must be aware of the potential for "irresponsible" revision. Irresponsible revision occurs when students are doing only as much as they must to get by. Instructors can avoid abuses of the system through the revision deadline policy or by using a U (unsatisfactory) grade signifying that the draft which has been submitted or resubmitted cannot be revised and resubmitted. The U grade sends the clear message that the student performance is inadequate.

The point of our attention to the syllabus in the preparatory workshop on portfolio evaluation is to make sure instructors understand the procedure and are able to communicate this understanding to their students. The syllabus serves as an informal contract between instructor and student; it is something both instructors and students must be able to live with.

Beginning the Semester

Once the semester begins, staff support shifts from formal workshops to staff meetings and frequent consultations between experienced portfolio users and novices. The most frequent problem instructors confront is the difficulty many students have adjusting to an ungraded system. At first, most students will express some anxiety, but this is mainly because of the novelty of the system. Soon these students will understand its purpose and benefits. Most respond very favorably to the idea that the drafts they submit can be revised and improved as a result of the feedback of peers and instructors and to the benefits of the learning space provided by portfolios.

There are students, however, who really cannot function without grades, and their special needs must be met. To help these students, we suggest the use of provisional grades. Students are invited to come to instructors during office hours, at which time student and instructor discuss the draft in question. A grade is provided based on the standards that will be invoked at the end of the semester. Instructors use this conference to move from evaluation to instruction. Students needing grades are often anxious and insecure about their writing, and the conference provides the perfect opportunity to offer individualized instruction and build confidence. These students and the opportunities they present are the subject of considerable discussion during informal staff meetings.

Another frequent concern is the need for instructors to send clear messages when responding to submitted drafts. Inexperienced instructors need help writing comments that reinforce what students have done well while pointing out what could and should be done before the paper can be considered strong writing. Practice on sample papers helps instructors develop strategies that allow them to be frank about the need for development and specific about revision while framing comments in supportive language that encourages students to strive to realize the potential of their papers. In addition, instructors must beware of creating unrealistic expectations in students about the quality of their writing, because such expectations will cause problems when portfolios are submitted.

A Midterm Conference

As an additional help to our students, we offer a midterm conference to discuss their progress in the course. These conferences come while there is still sufficient time for the student to withdraw from the class without jeopardy, if necessary, or to make arrangements to salvage the semester. Some instructors offer provisional grades. It must be stressed that these are only provisional grades and that the final grade can come only at the end of the semester with the portfolio.

The most important benefit of the midterm conference is the opportunity to turn some students around. These are the writers whose growth has been very flat and who seem poorly motivated. They depend on grades for motivation. Without grades they are driving toward mediocrity and need an awakening. While they would balk at the very prospect of earning a C, their performance thus far merits a C at best. They need to know, moreover, that doing a portfolio will not automatically result in a higher grade but that it is not too late to begin to work harder and improve their chances for success.

The key is moving from evaluation to instruction. In staff meetings we discuss the midterm conference as a potential motivating tool, a way if need be to shake students out of their complacency and drive them toward realizing their potential. In all instances, the midterm conference ends with the reminder that what has been said has been provisional and subject to change through increased effort and the understanding that comes with time and practice.

A Clearance Interview

The clearance interview is the final preparation for the portfolios. About four weeks before the end of the semester we distribute a comprehensive handout describing the portfolio system. The handout addresses the purpose of portfolio grading, the requirements for qualifying to do a portfolio, instructions on how to put the portfolio together, and end-of-semester deadlines.

The handout announces that anyone wanting to do a portfolio will have to meet with the instructor before a particular date. During this clearance interview, the instructor reviews the student's performance to make sure that the student qualifies in terms of attendance, participation, and the minimum number of accepted drafts. If a student qualifies, the instructor asks if there are any questions about the portfolio procedure. At this time the instructor may provide some needed information. For example, if a student is truly a C student, whose performance has been marginal all semester, the instructor should make clear how much improvement that student must make in the portfolio to break the C barrier. We try to be honest, to make sure some students are aware of the very long road they face. Students must be reminded that substantive improvement, not effort and good will, is the primary criterion by which we finally evaluate portfolios.[4] Given the workload of many college freshmen, and given the time and effort required to compile an effective portfolio, common sense suggests that marginal students are best advised to put their efforts elsewhere. They have already earned C's, and not doing a portfolio frees time to study for calculus or biology or whatever. Students generally appreciate such candor. And any information that can make students more realistic in their expectations makes the final interview easier on student and instructor alike.

The clearance interview allows instructors to remind students of one of the main points of the portfolio system—that students must assume responsibility for their writing and that the instructor's opinion and suggestions for revision must be considered along with peer critiques and, most important, in the light of the criteria for good writing that the students themselves have been developing all semester. When confronted with appeals for specific directions which the student can follow without thinking, the instructor must resist and turn the burden back onto the student: "How do you think the piece can be made better? What new information or argumentative angle do you see developing since you wrote the piece? What new information do the peer review sheets suggest the reader needs?" Instructors must beware of the tendency during the final steps of the portfolio system to undo all the semester's work by changing from respondent to director of revision, thereby allowing students to abandon responsibility for their writing.

Evaluating Portfolios

With the submission of portfolios begins a period of intense reading and evaluation. We discuss the process at a staff meeting where veterans of the system share their experience. Instructors must keep several things in mind when they begin to read portfolios. First and most important, they must remember that their role has shifted from respondent to evaluator. Definitions, revisions, and arguments must be considered for what they are, rather than what they could be after revisions. The examples of good writing the students present must be read in the light of the students' own definitions of good writing, and how well those definitions reflect the substance of the course. When reading the good writing examples, instructors should hold their responses until the end, writing only short summary comments stating whether they believe the examples and explanations of good writing are effective or not. Instructors should not explain deficiencies but should note them mentally in case students ask for explanations during the interview.

Reading the revisions is more demanding than reading the examples. Instructors report reading revisions two ways. Some read both the original and all the feedback on it, and then the revision, ultimately comparing the two to gain a specific sense of the changes made and their implicit purpose. Such close reading, however, is time-consuming and often counterproductive. Reading drafts encourages instructors to construct an "ideal" paper, the paper the instructor would write during revision. But only rarely does a student's revision reflect this "ideal" paper. Instructors report getting bogged down trying to understand why a writer followed some bad advice or took a tack that caused rather than solved problems in the paper. Such close reading ultimately reveals what the student did not learn, whereas the purpose of evaluation is to find and reward what the student *did* learn.

The second style of reading is the one preferred by most instructors. Instructors read only the revisions and consider whether they reflect what finished pieces of writing should be. Does each paper state and solve a problem? Does it address an audience effectively? Is it well-structured and logically sound and complete? Is it free from distracting errors or violations of writing conventions?

Instructors using the more holistic style of reading can focus on each revision as a paper in itself and judge whether it meets its own expectations, and how well it meets the specific criteria students, individual instructors, and the whole program have forged through the semester. Avoiding close comparison with drafts allows instructors to read papers and reward them for what they do rather than penalize them for what they did not do.

Allowing revisions and whole portfolios to exist on their own terms is an issue staff discuss specifically. Reading a portfolio honestly requires considerable forgetting. Beginning to read a portfolio with preconceptions about a student's ability and potential can lead to reading only to find evidence to confirm those preconceptions. This violates the purpose of the portfolio. Instructors need to read the portfolios to evaluate the writing in front of them, not to defend evaluations built up through the semester.

Since instructors will eventually have to respond to questions raised during the final interview, some shorthand notations in the margins will help serve as reminders of problems or strong points during the interview. Then, after the instructor has read the examples of good writing and found them effective or not, and read the revisions and judged them in the light of individual and program criteria, there is only the argument for a grade left to consider. The argument generally is easy to read and evaluate. Empty arguments betray inflated expectations. No one earns an A just for attending class and turning the work in on time. A's and B's come from the quality of the revisions and from individual growth. Arguments that address these issues specifically are successful and earn the student the grade requested. Arguments that do not address substantive issues receive little consideration. Students must be reminded while compiling portfolios that the final grade will be based on substance and quality as measured by the instructor. Submitting a portfolio does not *guarantee* a grade higher than a C.

The Final Interview

To prepare for the final interview, the instructor reviews the student's portfolio and decides finally whether the student has earned the grade requested. Experience indicates that about eight of ten students will have compiled portfolios that justify grades higher than C. On a successful portfolio, the instructor writes a summary comment congratulating the student on the quality of the portfolio and stressing one particular strength the student should continue to develop. Instructors mentally register one or two areas still needing development and mention these during the final interview. Occasionally instructors report raising a grade because a student has been too modest or conservative in his or her grade request. For students who have overshot the mark in their requests, brief summary comments explain the grades given. The comments note three or four instances where the grade arguments are faulty or incomplete, or the revisions or examples of good writing inadequate. Since this final review of each portfolio should come immediately before the meeting with the student, interviews should be scheduled to guarantee some private time to the instructor between students.

Interviews themselves are generally pleasant. Successful students often ask how they can continue their development, and instructors advise these students on which literature or writing course might be useful for them to take next. Instructors stress that the freshman course is the beginning, not the culmination, of students' development as writers, that they need more exposure and practice to realize their complete potential. We recommend specific courses and explain why they would be helpful.

Interviews with students whose arguments are inflated and unsuccessful vary. The students who knew they were asking for too much generally understand their final grades and are often able to explain their shortcomings as writers quite specifically. Sometimes students know that the problem is the normal time-lag between understanding and performance. They know they need more time and practice, and ask what their next course should be.

The other, less pleasant, interviews involve students who want to argue. Since instructors have already prepared rationales for their evaluations, they can respond specifically, and cut off those students who want to continue the argument for the sole sake of arguing. There are better ways to use time.

Of the steps in the portfolio procedure, the final interview is the most problematic. The interview demands interpersonal skills as well as competence in evaluating writing. Instructors using the portfolio system for the first time report a tendency to "cave in" during the final interviews. The source of the cave-in can be student pressure or the instructor's lack of confidence. These combine with the fondness for students that instructors develop through the highly interactive process of teaching writing and may lead to compromised standards.

For these reasons, inexperienced instructors are encouraged to discuss interviewing techniques with experienced portfolio users. A workshop where instructors discuss their experiences, anticipate and solve certain common interview problems, and simulate an interview or two helps new instructors build confidence. In addition, those using the portfolio with interview for the first time must have absolute confidence that the administration will support them by being available to solve problems when they arise, and by being ready to defend their decisions to students, parents, or higher administration should that become necessary.

Though the final interview sometimes causes a problem or two, it is the most effective way to complete a portfolio evaluation. The interview fosters communication between instructor and student, reinforcing the goals of the writing program as a whole.

Recapitulation

Portfolio evaluation is not an easy way to grade student writing. The procedure makes demands on the program, on the students, and especially on individual instructors. It requires an elaborate and individualized style of response/evaluation. It asks students to strive for excellence and long-term development rather than settling for the immediate gratification available through traditional grading. It demands the commitment of considerable time and psychic energy from instructors. But all of these challenges are manageable in light of the benefits that portfolio evaluation offers:

1. Portfolio evaluation reinforces a program's commitment to the teaching of writing as a process involving multiple drafting, and emphasizes the need for revision.

2. Portfolio evaluation establishes a writing course as an organic sequence of assignments, each building consciously upon the one before, and culminating in the development of "whole," process-aware writers rather than skillful hurdlers over unrelated individual assignments.

3. Portfolio evaluation establishes a writing environment rather than a grading environment in the classroom, encouraging instructors to become respondents providing feedback of the same kind as the feedback students get from their peers, though perhaps of a more sophisticated quality.

4. Portfolio evaluation encourages students to assume responsibility for the quality of their work. Students develop and apply a critical sense to their own writing, fostering the development of their potential and avoiding the problem of depending on the instructor for approval. This reflective critical sense may be the most valuable skill with which students leave the writing course. Portfolio evaluation creates independent writers and learners.

5. Portfolio evaluation frustrates the lowest-common-denominator, "get by," or survivalist mentality that some students bring into the classroom. They find no reward in doing only the minimum required. They are not competing with peers or contending with an instructor. Rather they must collaborate with peers and instructor and strive to realize their potential.

6. By postponing summative evaluation, portfolio evaluation avoids or at least tempers the frustration students feel when they do not succeed in early assignments, while allowing the instructor to begin a semester without feeling any pressure to compromise standards to avoid that frustration. The system encourages high standards from the start, thereby encouraging maximum development.

7. Most important, portfolio evaluation establishes an evaluation system that encourages instructors to focus on specific aspects of writing and to develop responsive skills. The system fosters a healthy trial-and-error attitude toward response/evaluation. Instructors and students confer and discuss reactions to writing rather than debating grades. Instructors individualize rather than pigeonhole students.

In sum, as reported by one novice instructor who had been particularly nervous about using the system, portfolio evaluation gives students and instructors "plenty of room to breathe and grow and enjoy the scenes along the way."

Notes

1. C. H. Knoblauch and Lil Brannon, "Teacher Commentary on Student Writing: The State of the Art," *Freshman English News* 10, no. 2 (Fall 1981): 1.

2. Nancy Sommers, "Responding to Student Writing," *College Composition and Communication* 33, no. 2 (May 1982): 152. Teacher response to student writing is a theme of two issues of *College Composition and Communication* (vol. 33, nos. 2 and 3, May and October 1982), in which a number of articles elaborate contemporary theory and practice.

3. James E. Ford and Gregory Larkin, "The Portfolio System: An End to Backsliding Writing Standards," *College English* 39, no. 8 (Apr. 1978): 950–55.

4. An excellent article to begin discussion of this crucial distinction between form and substance, work and quality work, is William Perry's "Examsmanship and the Liberal Arts: A Study in Educational Epistemology," in *Examining Harvard College: A Collection of Essays by Members of the Harvard Faculty* (Cambridge: Harvard Univ. Press, 1963).

How TAs Teach Themselves

Timothy R. Donovan
Patricia Sprouse
Patricia Williams
Northeastern University

As with many professions or trades, the teaching of English in American universities is organized much like the craft guilds of Western Europe during the Middle Ages: The masters, or professors, run the shop, or department, and supervise the apprentices, or graduate students. (We have our journeymen, too, but that is another matter.) The purpose of the guild was to control workmanship and to set standards, even price. And so, too, do English departments maintain accepted practices of teaching, testing, and scholarship.

The system has worked well enough, it could be argued, with the study and teaching of literature. The masters, drawing upon an abundant tradition of literary criticism, readily pass along the best that has been thought and known in the field to the apprentices, who may do likewise if they continue in the profession. But the system has not served the teaching of writing very well. Only recently have the masters thought and known about composition to the same extent, much less how to train their apprentices in it. Moreover, though apprentices may be designated teaching assistants, they usually "assist" no one and have full responsibility for conducting their classes from the outset. Finally, TAs who are literature majors (and this surely is a majority of our TAs) in reality have been learning one craft in their courses but performing another in their teaching.

As a result, whatever apprenticeship TAs may serve in composition is often to paper, not people. They are usually assigned a text, along with the trusty teacher's guide or department syllabus. A course description might advise on principles of rhetoric to be covered (e.g., unity, coherence, and transition) and types of writing to be required (e.g., exposition, description, persuasion). It is difficult to have a dialogue with paper, and TAs may change masters with every new book adoption.

Lately the situation has improved. As research in and respect for composition grows, more and more universities are developing real apprenticeships in the teaching of writing. Scholars conversant in rhetorical theory and pedagogy have instituted substantial programs of supervision for TAs. On the other hand, such efforts have not always led to the sophistication and stability expected. Philosophies of composition can be implanted in the program, only to wither during a term's worth of problems and paperwork. Textbooks are still introduced with a flourish one year, then discarded the next. Staff meetings always have the potential to be gripe sessions or military briefings, or both.

The crux of the matter may be that TAs are frequently not allowed sufficient involvement, much less partnership, in the development of materials for teaching writing. Typically, something is handed *down* to them, whether a book or outline, or the latest theory, writing assignment, classroom exercise, or method of grading. To be sure, most TAs are grateful for whatever help they can get; beginners, after all, must have some security and direction. But the departmental program, whatever it may be, will not, and cannot, consistently serve all their needs—or those of their students—as many TAs learn very quickly. Something happens in the classroom: They become teachers. They discover that there is more involved than imparting a codified body of knowledge, following a packaged lesson plan, or mimicking another teacher. They may see that, in teaching composition especially,

1. the timely assistance of the teacher during the composing process matters most. Instruction should be individualized and student-centered, focusing especially on the variables of invention, revision, and editing.

2. a teaching style begets writing style. Skillfully talking and listening to students about their writing is demanding, and the best of theories can fail in the hands of a poor teacher.

3. learning to write is very much a dynamic allowing for, even requiring, many pedagogical strategies. A creative teacher with a basic understanding of the writing process can devise a number of suitable classroom activities.

TAs, then, learn about teaching composition from their supervisors, but they also learn from their students, from each other, and from themselves, as well. By the time they settle into a semblance of a teaching style, however, they are preparing job résumés and are gone—and with them goes valuable expertise and materials.

The Resource Book

One instrument for turning their "growing period" to lasting advantage for the program and other TAs is the teaching resource book. We have in mind a kind of encyclopedia of activities, exercises, materials, strategies, and advice developed in the context of the given institution, embracing its philosophy and goals. A resource book may evolve in many ways, but our plan was fairly simple. Expertise would flow initially from the supervisor to the TAs in the form of seminars and workshops in the teaching of writing. Everyone would start from roughly the same premises. The TAs would take this expertise, filtered through their own intellects and personalities, into the classroom. Although given sample techniques, they would also be given sufficient latitude to modify or develop teaching strategies of their own. During the term they would keep a course log detailing their day-to-day experiences. After about a year, the logs would be collected, collated, and edited to form a resource book that would then be shared with all those teaching in the course. In this way, a theory of writing instruction, tempered by classroom practice, would be returned to the supervisor and the department with the virtue of having had hands-on application. Moreover, TAs would obviously have had a substantial role—not to mention stake—in the program.

We requested and received copies of course logs from ten new teaching assistants. Each entry in the log contained a description of a given activity, a statement of its purpose, an evaluation, and possible modifications and/or variations. Approximately thirty days of classroom activities, or as many as three hundred, were represented in all. We had expected to find a great deal of similarity and repetition from TAs working so closely within the same theoretical approach, but we found that they were developing various ways of presenting it in their classrooms. This variety presented some problems in compiling a sourcebook. Were we to edit and judge the "best" of the bunch? If so, would our decisions tend to reflect our own preferences, rather than the needs of the group as a whole? Would a broader spectrum provide more variety for others?

Immediately we saw the necessity of preserving all the various options when creating our sourcebook. We wanted to be representative rather than selective. We also wanted to arrange the selections in such a way as not to presume an order of presentation, since the course logs were chronological. Finally, we wanted to emphasize the fact that although several teachers may have used the same exercise, they had presented it with interesting variations. Our solution came from the very philosophy of the writing course itself.

Our formal approach to teaching writing depends upon five aspects of composition. (Here we are indebted to Thomas Carnicelli at the University of New Hampshire and Roger Garrison, Westbrook Junior College in Maine.) These are, in order, *content* (sufficient and pertinent information), *point of view* (purpose and audience), *organization* (the ordering of sentences, paragraphs, and the whole paper), *style* (diction and syntax), and *mechanics* (spelling, punctuation, and usage). This is our priority list in discussing composition with students and in reading their papers. It seemed natural to order the resource book according to these categories. There was no reason that TAs had to follow the priority list in lockstep on a week-by-week basis, but by filing exercises according to the categories of the priority list we had a way of indexing a great amount of material that could then be easily referred to.

Our book took shape quickly after this decision. Each section presented activities carefully described and assessed by the TA who had designed them. Most of the activities included several variations on the same theme, as well as some advice for teachers debating about using the activity. As illustrations of how a sourcebook works, here are a few entries describing the ways some TAs use the students' own writing to help them revise and understand the importance of revision in the writing process:

1. Select one or two student papers from the group of weekly essays turned in to be evaluated. You may choose the essays because they display some good points or illustrate some common errors. It is best to choose a "middle-of-the-road" paper—that is, a paper that can be discussed but not torn apart.

   If possible, have the paper(s) reproduced so that students may have copies before them. Read the paper aloud while the students follow along in preparation for discussing it. It is often best to begin with what the students liked or enjoyed about the paper. Encourage the students to point to particular passages in the paper and tell why or why not the passage is successful.

2. Have one or two students volunteer to read their papers aloud to the class. They should read the papers one paragraph at a time. The rest of the class should listen carefully and then discuss the paragraph that has been read. Have them concentrate on pointing to effective parts and sections that seem unclear. If students are confused, it may be a good idea to have the author reread certain parts. Encourage the author of the paper to join in the discussion. The author can preface the reading of a certain paragraph by explaining what he or she thinks is weak or strong. The audience can

agree or disagree accordingly. Have the students suggest improvements for places that seem vague or unclear.

3. Reproduce several sentences from class papers on a ditto and distribute the handout to the class. Have the students follow as the instructor reads the sentences one by one. Take a moment to have the students rate the sentences 1 (low) to 5 (high) in terms of clarity and effectiveness. Explain that the students must be prepared to justify their rating of each sentence. If there seems to be a general agreement that a sentence is weak or vague, revise the sentence on the board as a class.

4. Return papers to the class after they have been evaluated by the instructor. Have the students read over the comments for five to ten minutes. Ask the students if they understand the comments. Do they understand why a sentence is labeled awkward or vague? Ask several students to volunteer sentences or passages that have been marked on their papers. Ask the class if they agree with the teacher's comment. Why or why not? How could the problem be solved? From class discussion, derive a list of methods for improving vague or awkward sentence structures.

5. Take mimeographed copies of a piece of student writing into class. Read the paper aloud and have the students follow along. Do several in-class revisions of the same paper. Show the students that we revise for different elements in different ways. For the first revision, have the class concentrate on specific word choice and improving content; for the second, have the class concentrate on mechanics, looking for spelling and grammatical errors outstanding in the paper. Discuss each revision process thoroughly.

This exercise can be done as group work quite easily. Split the class into four groups. Assign each group a different revision task.

Group One: Revise for more specific words.

Group Two: Revise for clearer content. Where does the paper need to say *more* or *less*?

Group Three: Revise for organization. Is the paper ordered effectively? Could any of the sections be moved or paragraphs rearranged?

Group Four: Revise for mechanical problems. Have students refer to a handbook and dictionary as appropriate.

After ample time has passed, have a large class discussion by asking for reports from each of the four groups.

These seem to be well-conceived activities, but did they work? To some extent. Diverse evaluations by the TAs reflect their diverse experiences in the classroom and suggest matters to be considered by the supervisor and other teachers:

> Probably the best class so far. The students took the reading of one another's papers seriously and were quite helpful and perceptive in analyzing their fellow writers.

> The goals and objectives must be made very clear and specific. Otherwise students don't go into much depth and end up conversing.

> Boardwork and silent reading of papers work extremely well. The boardwork makes for a lively class. They like to watch that eraser go. The silent reading seemed to be pretty constructive.

> Students seemed eager to read each other's work. I looked over the comments later and saw they were very helpful and critical.

> It never ceases to amaze me how many students say that other students are not critical enough on their papers. I must remember to say this to the whole class next time.

> Students are generally too lenient on their peers. Also they talk of not being able to judge others' papers. Encouragement is constantly needed at first.

> It's not that we have to convince them that revision can be fun—to do that I would first have to convince myself—we have to convince them that revision can be worthwhile. Seeing examples of revision at work is really illuminating for some.

> Classes vary on how they respond to commenting on each other's papers. Some like it and do a good job, others find it less stimulating.

> Once they get going, they enjoy it. It helped them to read each other's papers. I'd say that I gave them too many guidelines. Three things to look for may be sufficient.

> I gave up on what might have been an effective discussion. I went too quickly through the handout. They lost consciousness on page two.

> I don't want to say it was a boring class, but out of twelve students who fell asleep, seven of them went into deep R.E.M. sleep, four of them snored so loudly that I could barely hear myself and one drooled all over his shirt.

> Personally, I think my revision workshop needs revision.

Clearly, then, no activity is guaranteed, and much depends upon the art of the teacher in implementing it. Still, the evaluations can help others foresee the difficulties.

The sourcebook is also helpful for TAs demonstrating specific principles of composition. Following, for example, are some attempts to focus on content that stress detail.

The "Empty" Paragraph

For this exercise the instructor distributes an "empty" paragraph—a paragraph lacking in specifics—to the students. Students are asked to fill in details in order to create a more interesting and distinct paragraph than the original. Most instructors feel it is important to have the students read the completed paragraphs aloud to illustrate the individuality that specific details lend to writing. Students come to realize that from one basic outline, many different compositions appear.

This is an "empty" paragraph often used by past instructors:

> He was a very unpleasant person—and not what I would call an honest person with anyone. His family didn't seem to care for him, and I didn't like much to look at him. He wasn't very pretty. As a boss he left a great deal to be desired. He defied the laws of good business in dealing with his customers. It's hard to see why they returned, except that he allowed them to charge things and they lived beyond their means.

Encourage the students to rewrite the paragraph using specific items to replace the general terms of the original. Explain to the students that they may wish to divide the paragraph into one or more paragraphs.

Some instructors choose to have students work in groups to write the paragraphs, which has advantages in large classes. Students collaborate on one paragraph for the final group presentation, reducing the number of paragraphs to be read aloud in class. In addition, group composing tends to eliminate student fears of reading their own writing aloud.

If the students write the paragraphs individually, it is possible to introduce a group element into the exercise another way. After the initial writing process, have the students exchange paragraphs and comment on the revisions. Have them answer directed questions at the bottom of the page. For example:

1. How has the writer improved on the original paragraph?
2. Select the detail you liked best and explain why it is effective.
3. At what point in the rewritten version could the writer use more details?

The Roommate's Desk

This exercise is a variation on "The 'Empty' Paragraph." Because of the shortness of the original paragraph describing a roommate's desk, this variation adapts well to boardwork. Begin this by putting the original paragraph on the board:

> My roommate's desk is a mess. It is covered with food, papers, and clothing. It is so cluttered that it took me three weeks to find my dictionary, which she borrowed a month ago.

Base a discussion on suggestions for improving the paragraph. Keep the students going even after they exhaust the more obvious possibilities. Encourage the students to increase the number of sentences.

It is possible merely to use this selection as a comparative model. Read the original paragraph and ask students if they think the paragraph is descriptive. Ask how they would improve the paragraph. After hearing various suggestions, distribute the following descriptive paragraph written from the original outline.

> My roommate's desk is a study in chaos. An electric typewriter caked with dust is the very decorative centerpiece. There is the remnant of a sheet of paper hastily torn from the carriage fluttering in the breeze from the open window nearby. The remains of three-week-old roses from her latest boyfriend droop from a Coke bottle. A box of Ritz crackers and a jar of Skippy peanut butter serve as one bookend for her textbooks; a stained coffee cup with a spoon in it and a jar of instant coffee serve as the other. A rolled-up sweatshirt leans wearily against a stack of overdue library books. A sheaf of notebook paper containing many scrawls is the rough draft for her term paper in history. The MLA handbook, a manual for writing term papers, is opened to the page on footnotes, where a McDonald's hamburger wrapper acts as a bookmark and a mustard packet lies atop the wrapper threatening to stain the page at any time. A jar which once contained Pond's cold cream now holds ten or fifteen pencils and a Bic ball point pen. Cigarette butts overflow in a large green ashtray shaped like the state of Florida. Under the ashtray is my dictionary, which she borrowed a month ago.

Since the rewritten paragraph is so rich in detail, it may serve only as an optional model to bring out when the class discussion has ended and the students are ready to leave. But it may also spark valuable discussions. How effective are the details in painting a picture? Are there too many details? Is the second paragraph more successful than the original? Why or why not?

Conclusion

We have presented these sections on revision and content for their own sake, but also to illustrate what TAs can do for themselves and in concert with others to shape a writing course. Moreover, by continually updating materials, TAs can have a living, working document that is part of *their* experience, not just of a distant author's or even of a sympathetic supervisor's. Each TA can use the classroom for curriculum research of this sort, rather than just surviving each class. And results can certainly be shared in some way with others, thus expanding the pool of support.

We have chosen the resource book as our vehicle for learning from each other. Our resource book is not the only solution by any means to the problems of shifting philosophies, texts, and staff, problems that extend to the whole profession. But it is a practical way of generating knowledge and enthusiasm, involving all who may wish to contribute, be they masters or apprentices.

Contributors

O. Jane Allen, assistant professor of English, teaches technical and professional communication at New Mexico State University. Her research interests include documentation and literature, and she has published essays in such journals as *Technical Communication, Modern Fiction Studies,* and the *Doris Lessing Newsletter.*

Charles W. Bridges is head of the Department of English, New Mexico State University, and is also director of the New Mexico State Writing Institute. With Ronald F. Lunsford, he is the coauthor of *Writing: Discovering Form and Meaning,* and has published in such journals as *College Composition and Communication, Freshman English News, The Arizona English Bulletin,* and *The National Writing Project Newsletter.*

Christopher C. Burnham, assistant professor of English, is director of freshman writing at New Mexico State University and is also codirector of the New Mexico State Writing Project. He has published in *The Journal of Basic Writing, The Journal of Advanced Composition, The Journal of Teaching Writing,* and *The National Writing Project Newsletter.*

Nancy R. Comley is director of freshman writing at Queens College of the City University of New York. She is coauthor with Robert Scholes of *The Practice of Writing,* and coeditor of *Elements of Literature* and *Fields of Writing,* and has published articles on composition and on English and American literature.

Don R. Cox, associate professor of English, is director of freshman writing at the University of Tennessee. He is the author of *Emblems of Reality,* and editor of *The Technical Reader* and *Sexuality in Victorian Literature,* and has published in such journals as the *Dickens Studies Newsletter,* the *Journal of Popular Culture,* and the *Comparative Literature Association Journal.*

Timothy R. Donovan is director of freshman writing at Northeastern University. With Ben McClelland, he is coauthor of *Eight Approaches to Teaching Composition.*

Richard C. Gebhardt is professor of English and assistant academic dean at Findlay College, where he coordinates the writing and general education programs and teaches courses in composition, literature, and the teaching of writing. He is the author of *Composition and Its Teaching: Articles from College Composition and Communication during the Editorship of Edward P. J. Corbett* and has published numerous articles in such journals as *College Composition and*

Communication, College English, the *ADE Bulletin, English Journal,* and *Freshman English News.*

Maxine Hairston is professor of English at the University of Texas at Austin and current chair of the Conference on College Composition and Communication. She is the author of *Successful Writing: A Rhetoric for Advanced Composition* and *A Contemporary Rhetoric.*

William F. Irmscher is professor emeritus of English at the University of Washington, where he was director of freshman writing for twenty-three years. He is also former chair of the Conference on College Composition and Communication. His publications include *The Holt Guide to English* and articles in such journals as *College Composition and Communication* and *College English.*

Richard L. Larson is professor of English at Herbert H. Lehman College of the City University of New York. He has published in such journals as *College English* and is currently editor of *College Composition and Communication.*

Ronald F. Lunsford is associate professor of English at Clemson University and is also codirector of the Clemson Writing Project. With Charles W. Bridges, he is the coauthor of *Writing: Discovering Form and Meaning,* and with Michael G. Moran, he is a contributing coeditor of *Research in Composition and Rhetoric: A Bibliographical Sourcebook.* In addition, he has published articles in such journals as *College Composition and Communication* and *Arizona English Bulletin.*

John J. Ruszkiewicz, associate professor of English, is director of freshman English at the University of Texas at Austin. He has published in *College English, College Composition and Communication,* and *English in Texas,* and is the author of *Well-Bound Words: A Rhetoric.*

Mary Jane Schenck is associate professor of English and assistant provost at the University of Tampa. Her publications include essays in *Comparative Literature, Romanic Review, Marche Romane,* and *Fabula.*

Patricia Sprouse is a graduate assistant in the department of English, Northeastern University.

Richard P. VanDeWeghe, associate professor of English, is the director of writing programs and director of the Center for Research in Rhetoric at the University of Colorado at Denver. He has published essays in such journals as *ADE Bulletin* and *The Arizona English Bulletin.*

Patricia Williams teaches business and technical writing in the department of English, Northeastern University.